ARAB FINANCIAL INSTITUTIONS

ARAB FINANCIAL INSTITUTIONS

NIDAL RASHID SABRI

Nova Science Publishers, Inc.
New York

For permission to use material from this book please contact us:
Telephone 631-231-7269; Fax 631-231-8175
Web Site: http://www.novapublishers.com

NOTICE TO THE READER

The Publisher has taken reasonable care in the preparation of this book, but makes no expressed or implied warranty of any kind and assumes no responsibility for any errors or omissions. No liability is assumed for incidental or consequential damages in connection with or arising out of information contained in this book. The Publisher shall not be liable for any special, consequential, or exemplary damages resulting, in whole or in part, from the readers' use of, or reliance upon, this material.

Independent verification should be sought for any data, advice or recommendations contained in this book. In addition, no responsibility is assumed by the publisher for any injury and/or damage to persons or property arising from any methods, products, instructions, ideas or otherwise contained in this publication.

This publication is designed to provide accurate and authoritative information with regard to the subject matter covered herein. It is sold with the clear understanding that the Publisher is not engaged in rendering legal or any other professional services. If legal or any other expert assistance is required, the services of a competent person should be sought. FROM A DECLARATION OF PARTICIPANTS JOINTLY ADOPTED BY A COMMITTEE OF THE AMERICAN BAR ASSOCIATION AND A COMMITTEE OF PUBLISHERS.

LIBRARY OF CONGRESS CATALOGING-IN-PUBLICATION DATA
Available upon request

ISBN: 978-1-60692-430-3

Published by Nova Science Publishers, Inc. New York

CONTENTS

Chapter 1	**Introduction**	**1**
Chapter 2	**Currency Systems in Arab Economy**	**9**
Chapter 3	**Arab Central Banks**	**13**
Chapter 4	**Commercial Banks**	**21**
Chapter 5	**Arab Development Funds**	**37**
Chapter 6	**Arab Insurance Companies**	**47**
Chapter 7	**Islamic Finance and Institutions**	**53**
Chapter 8	**Other Financial Institutions**	**65**
Chapter 9	**Conclusion**	**75**
References		**79**
Index		**85**

Chapter 1

INTRODUCTION

Today, the financial sector may be considered as the most mature sector compared to other economic sectors in the Arab economy. It uses local as well as foreign currencies in matter of exchanges and in measuring value of investment. The financial sector offers services through the process of buying money, financial instruments and securities or financial services in certain situation, and then reselling these money or financial instruments or services in another situation. The institutions that provide such services are called intermediary financial institutions, while the places of selling and buying money and financial instruments are known as financial markets. Accordingly, the financial sector includes besides the national currency, two major parts, financial markets and financial institutions, which have different merits, functions and mechanisms. Thus, this chapter is devoted to the financial institutions besides the issue of national currency in the Arab economy, while the next chapter is devoted to financial markets in the Arab economy.

Despite the fact that the financial sector is a new economic sector compared to other sectors such as the industrial and agricultural sectors, and it has mainly emerged and developed in the last century. But today the financial sector is considered as the most sophisticated and expanded sector in the world economy as well as in the Arab context, and it is expanding both vertically and horizontally as expressed by a variety of institutions and financial products. The financial sector activities work within a stated national legal framework. The legal framework is different from one state to another, which reflects the variety of the legal entities and financial instruments existing in the world economy as well as displaying the degree of maturity of such a sector. However, such variety mainly depends on the related laws which organize the activities of the financial sector. The types, merits, and mechanisms of the financial sector in any economy are determined based on the related laws, regulations and the jurisdiction system in general. For example, some activities, products, services, and producers belong to the financial sector may be permitted in one economy and not authorized in another economy.

The level of financial development in Arab states varies from one Arab state to another. It s mainly depends on one major institution which is banks, and one major market which is the stock market. The stock markets exist only in 15 Arab states; while the banks are exist in all Arab states, but with significant differences in the number of banks, values of deposits, granted credit, and owners' equity values. In addition, the degree of growth of financial sector is materialized by the non- banking financial institutions, currency system, financial and monetary policies, economic openness, and the economic growth. In a recent study issued by the IMF examined the development of the banking sector, regulation and supervision, financial openness, and institutional quality in the Arab economy and found that, some Arab states may be stated of the high level of financial development index including Bahrain, Lebanon, Jordan, Kuwait, UAE and, Saudi Arabia, while other states may be ranked at the second level of maturity including; Oman, Qatar, Tunisia, Egypt, and Morocco. However, Sudan, Djibouti, Yemen, Algeria and Mauritania were ranked at third level of financial developed, while Syria and Libya were ranked at the lowest level of the financial development including (Creane, et al. 2004). However, to examine and measure the level of financial sector maturity and reliability is a contradictory issue. For example, Elkelish and Marshall (2006) explored the applicability of modern financial structure theories in the United Arab Emirates and indicated that respondents are more likely to be driven by behavioral factors and influenced in their choices by business risk, while use of equity finance as a last financing resort.

To examine the importance and maturity of Arab financial sector compared to other regions and to the world economy, we can conclude that even the financial sector is the most important and the most growing sector in the Arab economy, but it is still in the early stage of development compared to the advancement occurred in the world economy as shown in Table No. 23.

It shows that the Arab financial sector formed about 2% of the world financial sector and about 12% of the emerging economy sector. The share of financial sector to the GDP was about 210%, which are still much less than the world ratio as recorded about 370% of the GDP. The most important part of the financial sector in the Arab economy as mentioned early is the banking sector and the stock market. However, it should be noted that the market capitalization of Arab stock markets decreased from the recorded value as $ 888 billion in 2006, leaving the banks as the leading financial sector, which formed about 12% of the emerging economies (AMF, 2006a and IMF, 2007a). The major shortage of the Arab financial sector comes from the tiny Arab bond sector, even after introducing the Islamic bonds besides the conventional bonds, especially in the corporate bonds which has minimum value compared to the emerging bonds markets.

Table 23. Comparison between Arab financial sector and the world financial sector in 2005 in $ billion

Financial Sector	Arab Economy	Emerging Economies	World Economy
Corporate bonds	27	1599.0	23,423
Government bonds	34	2,822.0	36,268
Stocks market capitalization	1,291	6,632.0	41,966
Bank Assets including development funds	1,100	9,432.8	63,473
Total: banks, stocks and bonds	2,452	20,485.8	165,130
Total as % of GDP	210%		370%

Compiled by author based on: IMF, 2007b, and AMF, 2006a.

The degree of development of the financial sector is mainly produced based on the economic growth as well as the related laws organizing the financial activities. The framework of the related laws organizing the financial sector may be classified in three groups:

First: The main framework of the legal entity of the Arab financial sector includes various levels as presented in Table No. 24. The first level is related to the social, economic, and political aspects which are considered as the base for building the legal fundamentals and enforcement institutes for any jurisdiction system. The general framework of articulating laws to organizing the financial transactions should reflect the economic and political views of the respective country. For example, if a country is directed towards the liberalization of its own economy, this leads to reorganizing the related laws and regulations to protect the concerned parties including national economy and local and foreign investors. The monetary policies also should be reflected in the related laws of financial activities, and should be accord with both financial institutions and markets policies and procedures. The merits of original of laws for an Arab state is a dominate factor in articulating the related laws of financial sector.

Table 24. Summary of legal framework organizing the Arab financial sector

Levels	Laws, regulations, codes and practices
First: Legal fundamentals	
	1. Political, social and economic aspects
	2. Monetary policies
	3. Original laws; (civil or common law) and "Sharaet" legislation
	4. Money and currency control laws
	5. Commercial laws
Second: Laws related to financial institutions	
	6. Banks laws (commercial, specialized, and Islamic banks)
	7. Central banks laws
	8. Insurance laws (Life and general)
	9. Money changers laws
	10. Insurance control laws
	11. Leasing financing laws
	12. Social securities agencies, public provident –pensions laws
Third : Laws related to financial markets	
	13. Corporate share laws
	14. Securities laws, and trading regulations,
	15. Government Securities Commissions' laws
	16. Stock exchanges' laws and by-laws
	17. Disclosures and reporting requirements,
	18. Brokers and membership requirements
	19. Insider trading laws
	20. Price limits regulations and margin regulations

The Arab original laws are belonging to either the civil law or common law besides the "Sharaet" legislation. For example, Jordan, Egypt, Lebanon and Morocco have a civil law with French original, while other Arab states have the common law due to the influence of British colony such as Bahrain.

The second group of laws belongs to organizing activities of financial institutions. The financial institutions are initiated and operated within the context of the national specialized laws; thus we find laws of banks, laws of insurance, laws of money changers, laws of leasing companies, and laws of provident and pension funds. In addition to that, there are laws to control all financial services such as laws of central banks, law of insurance commission to control the insurance activities. The financial institutions receive huge amounts of deposits, insurance premiums; thus the governments should impose strict rules to control and protect residents, local investors, depositors, insurance policy holders and foreign investors.

The third group of laws belongs to organizing aspects of the financial markets including the corporate law. The corporate law organizes types, features, and conditions of issuing the shares, which are traded in the world stock markets. However, the shares' merits are reflected on the efficiency and liquidity of the stock markets. The main aim of a corporate law is to maintain the balance between corporate governance, investor protection, and liquidity of stock market. The securities' laws organize the price and trading processes of the world stock markets including clearing and cash settlements procedures, listing requirements, delisting requirements, disclosure requirements, generally accepted accounting principles, and other requirements. The details and regulations of the above issues are related to securities' laws that vary from one jurisdiction to another. The stock exchanges' laws regulate the stock trading activities including: stock exchange by-laws, market organization, pricing regulations, cash settlements regulations, market supervision and authorization, arbitration rules, brokers and membership requirements, equity indices, index composition and weighting, calculation of index and methodology, and dissemination process of trading and prices. However, it should be noted here that there is an overlap between regulations and rules stated by securities laws and exchanges laws in some of the world jurisdictions. The majority of stock markets impose various regulations to prevent manipulations, protect investors, and to reduce volatility such as price limits, safe harbor rules, insider trading rules, investment protection rules and margin requirements for trading and cash settlements.

Finally, at the end of this section we would like to summarize the financial sector in the Arab economy as expressed by main groups and number of financial institutions and markets as existed in the Arab economy in June, 2007, which are categorized into two major groups as shown in Table No. 25.

First: the intermediary financial institutions: the first emerged intermediary financial firm was the moneychanger, that later grew to become commercial banks which offers the service of lending besides currency exchange. Other forms of financial institutions were emerged during the last century such as development funds, specialized banks, insurance companies, financial leasing corporations, and other financial institutions which offered various aspects of financial services.

Second: The financial markets which include both specialized markets as stock exchanges, currency and gold exchanges, and other markets to trade in

financial instruments such as treasury bills and currencies. The majority of the
Arab financial system is developed in the last five decades. However, few
financial markets were started as early at the beginning of the twentieth century as
will be presented in the next chapter.

Table 25. Summary of the Arab financial sector 2005- 2007

	No. of Institutions	Notes
First: Financial Insinuations		
Central Banks and AMF	23	
Commercial and Islamic banks	424	Including 57 foreign banks
Investment and specialized banks	101	
Arab Development funds	13	8 regional, and 5 national banks
Insurance companies	267	Life and general insurance firms
Social securities agencies, private and public pension funds	55	Pensions for government employees Pensions for private employees
leasing companies and others	Limited firms	
Brokerage firms	400	
Money changers	Many firms	
Second: Financial Markets		
Stock Exchanges	17	Equities: cash market Bonds: Treasury bills:
Government Securities Commissions	10	
Securities and Depository Centers	14	
Treasury bills through auctions		

Sources: compiled by the author based on: a- collected data, b- AMF, 2006a, c- GIAF, 2007.

The financial institutions include two groups; first, what is known as
depositary institutions such as banks and any financial institutions authorized by
the national related laws to receive deposits from customers, thus need more
governmental control to protect thousands of depositors, and the second group is

known as contractual financial institutions which receive periodical installments on return for different compensations based on stated conditions such as the case of life and general insurance, and pension funds. The contractual firms have no rights to receive funds from customers in the form of deposits, but may be received for long term investment and compensation such as in case of pension funds. The financial institutions in the Arab economy include 21 central banks, 324 commercial banks, 101 specialized banks and 100 Islamic banks, and 13 development funds in 2006 as shown in Table No. 25. Of the total, about 57 banks are foreign banks operated in the Arab states (AMF, 2006a). For Arab funds, there are about eight regional funds owned fully or partially (more than 50%) by Arab states, and five developed funds owned by Individual Arab oil states.

In addition, there are about 267 insurance corporations working in general insurance, reinsurance, and life insurance. The majority are working only in general insurance, while a small part of the operated insurance corporations work in reinsurance and life insurance. Pension and provident funds are also existed in the Arab economy, which work beside the retirement government programs. However, the majority of pension funds are owned by the governments of the Arab states.

The money changers represent a substantial part of the Arab financial institutions, even this group work in the form of small sole firms, partnership firms, private corporations, and with few public corporations. Mutual funds also now existed in the Arab economy which divided it is own capital to equal shares and to be sold to investors.

The Arab financial institutions are mainly organized in public corporations and operated under national regulatory bodies such as the central banks, national insurance supervisory authorities or commissions, and capital market supervisory authorities or commissions. In addition, they are organized in unions, federations, associations, societies and syndicates at national and Arab levels. For example, at the national level almost all financial institutions in all Arab states are organized to serve and defend their own interests. Accordingly, we find the Insurance Federation of Egypt, the society of banks in Palestine, the syndicate of Lebanon money changers, Emirates Banks Association and so on in each of the Arab states. For Arab level, there are the Union of Arab banks, the General Arab Insurance Federation, the Council for Arab Central Banks, and the Arab committee for Banking Supervision. In this regard, we find the Arab coordination among the financial institutions is more active and materialized than existed in other economic sectors. In addition, other financial institutions may have associations at other regional levels or at the world levels.

For financial markets, there are about 17 stock markets existing in 15 of the Arab states since in UAE there are three stock exchanges, 15 of them are members of Arab monetary fund. In addition, there are also various Government Securities Commissions and national securities depository centers and cash settlements agencies. The rest of this chapter will be devoted to discuss the mentioned Arab financial institutions in more details, after presenting a section regarding the currency issue in the Arab economy.

Chapter 2

CURRENCY SYSTEMS IN ARAB ECONOMY

The majority of the currency regimes of Arab countries have a constant rate against $US including UAE, Jordan, Bahrain, Saudi Arabia, Oman, Qatar, and Kuwait. The rest of the Arab currencies witnessed significant devaluation in their values against $US between 1994 and 2004 such as in Egypt, Sudan, Mauritania, Yemen, Libya, Tunis, and Algeria currencies. Some of these currencies lost more than 50% of their values against USD in the last decade including Sudan, Yemen, Mauritania, and Libya (AMF, 2006a). The Arab currencies may belong to various exchange rate systems as shown in Table No. 26. The majority adopted a pegged exchange rate against USD, Libya adopted an exchange rate against a composite or SDR (Special Drawing Rights), while Algeria, Sudan, Mauritania, Tunisia, and Yemen adopted a managing floating system. In addition, The Arab Gulf Cooperation Council members including Bahrain, Kuwait, Oman, Qatar, Saudi Arabia, and the United Arab Emirates have agreed to establish a monetary union by the year 2010 with a single currency pegged to the U.S. dollar.

However, the announced exchange rate arrangements may be different than practices such as that in Egypt, Lebanon, and Syria.

To select a relevant system for exchange rate is a contradictory issue, because every system has both advantages and disadvantages regarding major elements of the economy and its impact in macroeconomic policy as well as the economic performance. Many studies discussed this issue regarding Arab economy and have non- collusive results.

Table 26. De Facto exchange rate arrangements for the Arab states as of July, 31, 2006

Arab States	Exchange Rate Arrangements
Djibouti	Currency board arrangements
Bahrain	A fixed arrangement against USD
Saudi Arabia	A fixed arrangement against USD
Egypt +	A fixed arrangement against a single currency
Syria =	A fixed arrangement against a single currency
Qatar	A fixed arrangement against USD
Oman	A fixed arrangement against USD
Iraq +	A fixed arrangement against a single currency
Jordan	A fixed arrangement against a single currency: USD
Kuwait	A fixed arrangement against USD
Lebanon +	A fixed arrangement against a single currency: USD
UAE	A fixed arrangement against USD
Libya	Arrangements against a composite or SDR
Morocco	Arrangements against a composite of currencies
Algeria	Managed floating
Sudan	Managed floating
Mauritania	Managed floating
Tunisia	Managed floating
Yemen	Managed floating
Palestine	No Currency

+The regime operating de facto in the country is different from its de jure regime
= Maintains arrangement involving more than one foreign exchange market

Source: IMF, 2007b.

For example, Ghosh et al., (1997) argued that using the pegged exchange rates by the majority of Arab states may has the advantage of controlling and lower inflation, but they are also correlated with slower productivity growth. Abid and Davoodi (2003) reported that the choice of an exchange rate regime has not always been appropriate in the region and such states have had a tendency to delay adjustment of pegs in the presence of clear real exchange rate appreciation. Jbili and Kramarenko (2003) argued for the need for greater exchange rate flexibility, as the economies become more diversified and more integrated into the world economy. While Benbouziane, and Benamar (2007) whom tested the impact of exchange regime on inflation, nominal money growth, foreign direct investment, exports, imports and GDP growth reported that, there were significant impacts in the short run, while in the long run, the exchange rate regime has no effects on the economic performance in MENA countries. Hakim and Neaime,

(2005) reported that currency depreciation will lead to losses in Arab banks. Tawadros (2007) tested the hypothesis of long-run money neutrality for Egypt, Jordan, and Morocco and found that the money is neutral in these three economies suggesting that the anti-inflationary policy should be merged by the monetarist school to curb inflation.

The issued national currency is supposed to be covered partially by foreign securities, bonds and gold based on the annual issued notes and the reevaluation of the reserved gold value and according to the hold accounts with the IMF. For example, the structure of the Egyptian currency cover at end of June 2006 was 92% as government bonds and 8 % as gold, in which the value of gold reached about $ 1 billion at the end of 2006 (CBE, 2006). Another example, the value of deposited gold in the IMF belongs to Saudi Arab Monetary Agency was about 67,390,878 Saudi Riyals as part of the Saudi Arabia subscription to the International Monetary Fund and as currency cover of 0.20751 grams per one Saudi Riyal (SAMA, 2006).

The circulated currency represents a part of what is known as money supply or domestic liquidity, the other parts include types of customers' accounts deposited in banks working inside the national state. The accounts include the current accounts known as checking or demand accounts, the saving accounts and the term- deposit accounts which are the most significant accounts as expressed by accumulated values. The accounts may be held by residents and non- residents, and usually opened in local and foreign currencies. Thus the issued national currency hold by public and circulated outside the central bank plus the value of current accounts in the local currency in banks operating in the state represent what is known as M1 of the money supply, if the quasi money added which include local savings and term deposit accounts and foreign currency deposits will produce what is known as money supply M2. The M3 also may be calculated if we consider the issued bonds and treasury bills. The ratio of circulated money to the total money supply is based on the maturity of banking and financial systems in the respected state and the share of other payment instruments in the economy. For example, the share of circulated currency is about 13% of the total money supply in Egypt, 5% in Qatar, 2% in Lebanon, and 30% of the total money supply in Sudan (CBE, 2006; QCB, 2006; BDL, 2006 and CBS, 2006). However, in general, there are four major payment instruments including:

- Money in circulation outside the central bank, including notes and coins, the share value of coins is about 1% of the total circulated currency. The value of circulated money is depending on the customs of inhabitants using other payment instruments and the purchasing power of the currency. The equivalent value of circulated national currency was $ 1 billion in Qatar, 12.3 billion in Egypt, $ 1 Billion in Lebanon, and $ 2.7 billion in Sudan, $ 7.3 billion in Iraq, and $ 2.3 billion in Kuwait (CBE, 2006; QCB, 2006; BDL, 2006 CBK, 2006; CBI, 2006, and CBS, 2006).

- The value of check payments issued in both local and foreign currencies is much higher than the value of circulated money and may be considered as the first payment instrument in the developing economy expressed by value compared to cash money. For example, the value of checks passed the clearing house of the Kuwait central bank was about 31.6 billion during the 2006 (CBK, 2006), which was about 14 times of the circulated money in the Kuwaiti economy for the same period

- Card payments and electronic transfers including credit cards, debt cards, charge cards and points of sales cards which are used in payments. The debt and credit cards are the most used cards in the Arab economy compared to other cards. The use of points of sales cards depends on the number of banks that use the system and the number of contracts signed with merchants.

- The electronic transfer system of payments, which will be explored later in the book.

Chapter 3

ARAB CENTRAL BANKS

The central bank is the bank of the state, owned completely by the government, but has legal, managerial and financial independent status and is separated from the governmental budget. Central banks have many objectives and functions as stated in their respective laws. The main target of the central bank is to manage the monetary policy of the country. However, if we examined the related laws of Arab central banks, we find that the stated objectives are similar by a few varieties. The majority stated some of the following objectives as the main aims of the Arab central banks;

- To issue national currency including banknotes and coins and state specifications and controlling on currency circulations. The central bank is the sole authorized organization that has the privilege of such right in this regard. The issuance of currency should be backed by either gold or/and foreign bonds, securities and foreign currencies; and currency issued appears on liability side of the balance sheet of the central bank. However, in USA, President Nixon declared that the issuance of US currency only to be backed by the trustworthy in the government of the US since 1971. Accordingly, there are no backup gold or foreign currencies and securities equally to the value of the circulated US currency.
- To keep and mange the government reserves including the reserved gold and foreign currencies deposited locally or in international banks and organizations including their subscriptions in the IMF in the form of gold or in SDR. The SDR is the IMF currency which is an account unit uses in transactions between the IMF and the world member states.

- To represent the government in the related international institutions such as the IMF, the World Bank, and the Bank of settlement.
- To represent the national government in the related region institutions such as the Arab Monetary Fund and the Arab develop funds and other specialized institutions.
- To supervise, control and assure the stability of banking system's activities including equity requirements and liquidity regulations.
- To license new private banks and money changers in the state as well as to cancel licenses and impose punishments in case of violation of the related laws on the depositary institutions.
- To supervise the process of liquidation of banks or foreign branches when it is required and according to the related laws.
- To prepare and publish the national economic and financial formal statistics.
- To state and control credit ceiling and interest rate policies, and to examine the cost of credit offered to national residents.
- To monitor and maintain inflation stability in the national economy.
- To supervise and manage the national payments system.
- To regulate foreign exchange trading and monetary foreign currency flows.
- To determine exchange rates between national currency and other currencies on a daily basis.
- To conduct the interrelationship between banks working in the state, including manual or electronic clearing service of checks and other forms of payments.
- To issue, mange and contract the government public debt including issuing of treasury bills, bonds, local and foreign loans.

The establishment of Arab central banks came immediately after the independence of the respective states or thereafter. Accordingly; we find that the majority of the central Arab banks were established between 1950 and 1975. The central banks of Iraq, Morocco, Syria, Saudi Arabia, and Tunisia were established in the fifties, while the central banks of Algeria, Egypt, Jordan, Kuwait, and Lebanon were established in the sixties. The reset of central Arab banks were established later as shown in Table No. 27. They were usually emerged and came as substitute of currency committees or currency boards, which used to order issuing the national currencies. Some of the Arab central Banks were first established as monetary agencies and later on changed to central banks such as in case of Bahrain and Qatar. The official name of the central banks in the Arab economy ranged from the central bank such as in case of Egypt, Jordan, Libya, Qatar, Oman and Tunisia, or the Bank of the name of the state, such as in case of Lebanon, Morocco, Sudan, and Algeria, or as monetary authority or agency such as in Saudi Arabia and Palestine.

Table 27. Summary of the Arab central banks and their total assets in $ Billion in 2005-2006

Arab States	Started Operation	Official Name	Total Assets
Jordan	1964	Central Bank of Jordan	2.0
Egypt	1961	Central Bank of Egypt	62.6
Bahrain	1973	(Bahrain Monetary Agency)	1.1
	2006	Central Bank of Bahrain	
Iraq	1956	Central Bank of Iraq	29.4
Kuwait	1969	Central Bank of Kuwait	10.4
Libya	1956	Central Bank of Libya	61.7
Lebanon	1964	The bank of Lebanon	27.8
Morocco	1959	Bank of Morocco	20.5
Oman	1975	Central Bank of Oman	4.7
Qatar	1973	Qatar Monetary Authority	5.4
	1993	Qatar Central Bank	
Syria	1956	Central Bank of Syria	17.5
Saudi Arabia	1952	Saudi Arab Monetary Agency	150.8
Sudan	1960	Central Bank of Sudan	6.9
Palestine	1994	Palestinian Monetary Authority	0.6
UAE	1980	Central Bank of UAE	21.9
Yemen	1971	Central Bank of Yemen	5.0
Mauritania	1973	Central Bank of Mauritania	0.8
Tunisia	1958	Central Bank of Tunisia	
Algeria	1962	Bank of Algeria	
Somalia	1975	Central Bank of Somalia	

Source: Compiled by Author based on the respected Annual reports of the Arab central banks 2005 -2006.

The capital of the Arab central banks is relatively small compared to the capital of the Arab development funds, and it is increasing annually, due to transferring part of the annual profits to the capital reserves. In addition, the total assets of the central banks are relatively high due to the holding foreign assets and government bonds. Thus the total assets of the Arab central banks ranged from less than one billion as in case of Palestinian Monetary Authority and central bank of Mauritania, to $ 1.1 billion for the Bahrain central bank, to $ 2 billion for central bank of Jordan, to $ 4.7 billon for central bank of Oman, to $ 5 billion for central bank of Yemen, to $ 5.2 billion for Qatar central bank, to $10.4 billion for central bank of Kuwait, to $ 17.5 billion for Syria central bank, to $ 20.5 billion for Bank of Al- Maghreb, to $ 21.9 billon for central bank of UAE, to $ 27.8 billion for central bank of Lebanon, to $ 29.4 billion for central bank of Iraq, to $ 61.7 billion for Libya central bank, to $ 62.6 billion for the central bank of Egypt and $ 150.8 billion for Saudi Monetary Agency.

The major items of the Arab central bank assets include the hold gold in the national treasury and in the IMF, the SDR balance in the IMF, cash and deposits hold in foreign banks for the account of the central bank, investment in foreign bonds and treasury bills, investment in local securities, portfolios, loans to local banks, loans to public and government, and fixed assets including land, properties and other assets. The liability items of the central bank include: credit balances and short term loans and local banks' current accounts hold as voluntary or obligatory by the central bank, and issued treasury bills. The second major group of the central bank liabilities is related to the national currency issued directly by the central bank or through local banks. The issued currency included both notes and coins, which are put in circulations, and are not printed and kept in inventory. The third group of items includes term deposits accounts, medium and long term loans belong to commercial and foreign banks, deposits belong to other financial institutions such as insurance firms and pension funds, the net issued government bonds and the balances belong to government agencies. The fourth group item belongs to capital and reserves of the central banks including the paid capital, accumulated reserves, and the transferred annual earned income. In addition, the central banks may manage general or special accounts and funds on behalf of the government.

The Arab central banks accomplish considerable annual profits, which are produced from investing hold deposits from national banks, revenues from government investment and securities, net profit from foreign currency trading and transactions, commissions and fees, and returns from portfolio. For example, The Saudi Arabia Monetary agency accomplished $ 210 million in 2006, the Central Bank of Kuwait accomplished about $ 241 million in 2005-2006, and the Bank of Sudan accomplished net income about $ 140 million in 2006 according to their annual reports. The annual net profit of central banks may be used in various ways according to the central banks' bylaws, and the government policies and decisions, such as:

- To be added to the general reserve of the bank, and becomes a part of the central bank capital and reserves.
- To be transferred to treasury account, and /or to be used to cover the shortage in the government budget.
- To finance purchasing of land and construction of new premises to government purposes.
- Contribution to the government retirement funds and social security programs.
- To be invested in local and foreign securities.

However, the major function of central banks is to control banking operations and monitoring regulations of activity, risk, capital adequacy, and liquidity of banking service, as presented in Table No.28. The presented measures are stated by the Palestinian Monetary Authority, which presents an example of the duties of central bank in the Arab economy. The table shows the various measures which have been set to control types and limits for major activities of the banking system in order to assure minimum risk as well as to serve the national economy; this includes mentoring investment, fixed assets, securities, and loans transactions. For risk measures, various maximum levels were stated regarding credit granted to one customer (assets concentration), ownership in a capital company, and trading in foreign currencies. In addition, detailed regulations are stated to organize the allowances for nonperforming loans.

Finally, for adequacy of capital, there are various measures including the minimum ratio of the adjusted ownership of the weighted risk assets, a minimum amount of paid capital, and an annual 10% of the net profit to be added to the obligatory reserves up to be equivalent to 100% of the paid capital (Sabri and Jaber, 2006). The last measure is applied for all corporations by the applied corporate law.

The central banks in Arab states have almost similar control procedures with some differences regarding the stated ratios of the control aspects, especially in the case of activity and risk measures. However, the majority of Arab central banks have largely or somewhat independent status from government with less independent status in Syria, Tunisia, Libya Mauritania and Egypt. The majority of the central banks liberated interest rate and credit measures, but they kept imposed regulations to monitor general situation (Creane, et al., 2004).

Table 28. Control measures used by PMA to supervise operations of banks in Palestine

Aspects	Measures	Ratios
Activity measures		
Ownership of fixed assets	Fixed assets to total assets	25%
Ownership in securities	Securities to total assets	25%
Investment outside Palestine	Total investment to deposits	65% maximum
Granting loans and credit	Credit to deposits	40% minimum
Un-permitted activities	Stated by law of banks	
Permitted upon permission	Trading in options Granting loans to non-residents Investment in foreign securities	
Adequacy of Capital		
Adequacy	Adjusted ownership to weighted risk assets	10% to 12%
Minimum capital requirements	Paid capital	5 to 20 US$ million
Regulatory reserves	up to 100% of paid capital	10% of profit
Liquidity		
Liquidity ratio	Current assets to deposits	25% as minimum
Cash ratio	Cash to deposits	4% as minimum
Risk		
Ownership in a capital company	Value share to capital	10% maximum
Credit granted to one customer	Value to capital	10%- 15% maximum
Trading in foreign currencies	Short or access in foreign currency positions to owners' equity	5%
Allowance for bad loans	Due loan values based on due date of loan (180 to 360 days)	20% to 100%
Cash to be deposit in the PMA as minimum legal reserves	Based on deposits and credits	6% to 15%

Sources: Sabri and Jaber (2006) based on PNA law 1998, PNA, Law of Banks of 2002, and various circulars issued by the Palestinian Monetary Authority (1995-2004).

The Arab central banks have to deal with three major regional and international financial institutions among other institutions and governments, in order to implement their stated objectives. First; the Arab monetary fund which was established in 1976 and located in the Abu Dhabi in UAE, which is owned by all Arab states, in order to settlement of current payments between member States, to work towards the creation of a unified Arab currency and to provide technical assistance to banking and monetary institutions in member States as stated by the bylaws of the fund. The total assets of AMF were about 1.3 billion Arab Dinar (AD = $4.3 in 2006). The coordination between Arab central banks is organized also through the AMF using various channels including periodical meetings for the Arab central banks governors, the activities of the council of Arab centers banks, and Arab committee for banking supervision, which was established to enhance and coordinate the supervisory function in Arab banks, and to follow the adaptation of Basel regulations governing the capital adequacy on Arab banks (AMF, 2005).

The second institution is the Bank for International Settlements (BIS) which was established in 1930 as an international organization and located in Basel of Switzerland. It aims to foster international monetary policies and financial cooperation; it served as a bank for the world central banks, and act as an agent in connection with international financial operations and settlements of payments. It also, helps the world central banks in managing their foreign exchange reserves. The total assets of the BIS is about SDR 220 billion in 2006 (SDR = $1.52) according to the annual report (BIS, 2006b). The third world institution is the International Monetary Fund (IMF) which includes 185 state members, and was established in 1945 and located in Washington D. C. It aims to promote international monetary cooperation and exchange currency stability, to maintain orderly exchange arrangements among members as stated by its law. The total assets of IMF were about $ 318 billion in 2006 (IMF, 2006d). The world states put part of their reserves from gold and foreign currency in the IMF disposal and as a part of their contribution in the SDR deposits system.

Finally, it should be noted at the end of this section, that the role of the central banks in the developed economy is so significant regarding the general economic issues and policies, but in the Arab economy, the role of central bank is to concentrate on monitoring the banking system, managing the government accounts and assets and to carry out the currency issuing aspects, rather than formulating the national economic polices and strategies. This is due to the shaky independency status for the majority of Arab central banks. Moreover, the central banks may state the interest rates for both deposits and loans for national currencies, but gradually the central banks abandon this role and left it to the commercial banks and to the market forces. This new situation also excludes the role of the central banks partially from interfering to reduce inflation and to direct the national economy in general.

Chapter 4

COMMERCIAL BANKS

Introduction: The banking sector offers different banking services including granting loans and other credit facilities, accepting customers' deposits, processing checks and transferring funds among other services. The major activity of banks is granting loans and other credit facilities such as overdraft services, discounting bills and financing imports. The majority of the central Arab banks stated in their related laws the minimum capital for their national banks as well as for foreign branches. The role of the paid capital of the bank is to serve the following purposes:

- The organization's function of banking activities and to cover the establishment cost of the bank.
- The operational function of paying current and operational expenditures up to produce enough revenues.
- The third function is the most important one, which is related to the protection of depositors and other creditors; it offers the minimum level of protection in case of liquidity of the bank.

The Arab banking sector is the most important sector in the Arab financial system as expressed by owners' equity including the paid capital and reserves, which reached about $ 92 billion in 2005. The total assets of the Arab banks have reached over $ 1 trillion in 2005, half of the amount had been offered as loans to serve the Arab economy as presented in Table No. 29. The total value of deposits was more than $ 600 billion. The ratio of total bank deposits formed about 56% of the GDP for the Arab economy in general. The granted loans were directed for both private and public projects (AMF, 2006a).

Table 29. Summary of the Arab banking system as exited at the end of 2005

Financial Indicators; Values	$ Billion
Owners' equity (Capital and reserves)	92
Loans and credits offered to public and private	576
Deposits	601
Total Assets	1043
Loans and credits to private sector	412
Term and saving deposits	372
Current deposits	176
Financial Indicators; Ratios	Ratio
Ratio of private loans to GNP	39%
Ratio of private credit to deposits	69%
Ratio of deposits to GDP	56%
Number of banks	470

Source: AMF, 2006a.

In addition, there is a continuous improvement of Arab banking sector in the last decade. For example, the owners' equity of Arab commercial banks increased 26% from 2004 to 2005 and about 18% for the granted loans, 16% for the deposits, and 18% of the total assets. In addition, the most expanding period for the Arab banking businesses was in the period between 2000 and 2006. For example, the total deposits in Arab commercial banks have been increased about 77% from 2000 to 2005 (AMF, 2006a; and OAPEC, 2006). The major increase has occurred mainly due to the increase of oil prices; which leads to increase the governments' revenues.

However, the importance and size of the banking system differs between the Arab states. For example, two thirds of the Arab banking deposits value is located in Saudi Arabia, UAE, Egypt, Lebanon, Kuwait, and Morocco. In addition, only 10% of total Arab banks are conducting the majority of banking activities as expressed by deposits, loans and total assets. For example, 3 Jordanian banks, 2 Kuwaitis, 4 Egyptians, 2 Bahraini, 5 Lebanon, 3 Moroccan, 3 Oman's, 3 Qatari, 6 Saudi Arab, 5 UAE and 4 Yemenis banks formed the majority of Banking activities in the Arab economy (AMF, 2006a; and Creane, et al., 2004). The top ten Arab funds are located in the Arab Gulf states, Egypt and Jordan. They have formed about 30% of the total owners' equity of all Arab banks, 23% of the granted loans, and 30% of the deposits and 25% of the total assets. In addition, the top 100 banks formed 75% of total banks assets and reached $ 802 billion, 71% of the total banks credit, and 72% of the deposits. The top ten Arab banks have assets ranged between $18 billion and $ 39 billion for each, and the granted loans and credits ranged between $ 20 billion and $5.6 billion for each. The collected deposits by the top ten Arab banks ranged between $ 28 billion and $ 9.4 billion in 2005.The Arab top banks ranked among the world top 1000 banks between Number 109 and number 231 as shown in Table No.30 (UAB, 2006), which means that in spite of the importance of these banks, it is still limited compared to the top world banks such as Citigroup, JPMorgan Chase, Bank of America, and HSBC which have equities over $100 billion for each and have total assets of over $ one trillion for each.

Table 30. Top Arab ten banks in 2005 and their ranks among the world banks in $ billion

Top Arab Banks	Rank in region	Rank in world	Assets	Credits	Equity	Deposits
National Commercial; SA	1	109	39	20.1	5.8	28.0
SAMBA; SA	2	162	29	16.7	3.4	22.7
National bank; Egypt	3	377	27.7	11.2	1.1	23.2
Arab bank; Jordan	4	202	27.5	12.4	3.9	17.6
Al-Rajahi Bank; SA	5	152	25.3	21.4	3.6	19.0
Gulf International; Bahrain	6	280	22.9	7.2	1.7	9.4
National Abu Dhabi; UAE	7	246	22.8	14.0	2.0	16.2
Riyad Bank; SA	8	176	21.4	12.2	2.9	14.1
National bank; Kuwait	9	231	21.2	11.5	2.7	13.6
Baanqu Misr; Egypt	10		18.5	5.6	0.6	16.1

Sources: UAB (2006) United of Arab Banks Journal (Issue 309; August, 2006); 275-280.

Finally, the Arab banking sector is on the top of Arab financial sector, but at the same time it is still at moderate size compared to the world economy. For example, the banking lending from Arab banking system represents only 8% of the developing economies according to the World Bank report (World Bank, 2006a) as shown in Table No. 31.

Types of Arab banks: In general, there are so many types of banks operated in the world economy. However, some of these types are authorized to work in some countries, while they are not permitted in others according to the related rules and regulations. The types of banks are so different in their ownership, legal entity, stated purposes, regulations, major operations, degree of specialty, nationality, the organization structure, major merits, costumers' target, and other bases as shown in Table No. 32. Which indicated a list of types of banks in the world economy, and if they are existed in the Arab economy as in 2007.

Table 31. Summary of capital flows in Middle East and Northern Africa in $ Million in 2005

Capital Flows	Values in Million in 2005	Total developing countries	Ratio of Developing countries
Cross-border loans flows	12,151	198,135	8.0%
Private debt flows	4,600	191,600	2.4%
Bonds flows	5,400	130,900	4.0%
Bank Lending	15,700	198,100	8.0%

Source: World Bank, Global Development finance, 2006a.

The table shows that banks may be classified in various forms; First classification is based on ownership, which includes public state owned banks and private banks, and banks with joint ownership. Today, the majority of the existed banks in the world economy are private owned banks. In the Arab economy, the state ownership of bank assets ranges from 95% for Algeria, 90% for Libya, 62% for Egypt, 38% for Morocco, 40% for Tunisia, 37% for UAE, 48% for Qatar,18% for Kuwait (World Bank, 2006c). The public banks were the only banks existed in Algeria, Iraq, Libya, Syria and Egypt before privatizations programs. In Jordan and Mauritania there are only private banks, while the rest of Arab states have both private and public banks and governments holding significant shares of various private banks. The banks may be conventional or Islamic banks based on dealing with interest rate. All of the Arab states may have both types of banks, with exception of Sudan which has only Islamic banking system in the Northern of Sudan, while the conventional banks is permitted in the Southern of Sudan.

The public corporation banks is the main legal entity of banks existed in the Arab economy, while other legal entities such as cooperative, credit union, public and private corporations are either not existed or rarely found in some of Arab states. Some banks such as mutual saving banks, loan associations, small microfinance banks and mortgage banks are not existed. The majority of the Arab states have at least one specialized bank such as in agriculture, industry, real estate and housing banks. In some economies the bank may be operated only through one branch such as in few states in USA, while the majority of banks in all over the world including the Arab economy work within the system of central administration and various branches located inside and outside the home. Banks also may be registered as national, foreign or offshore banks. The majority of Arab states permit foreign banks, while the offshore bank is operated in few Arab states such as in Bahrain, which formed about 83% of Bahrain banking system compared to 12% for commercial banks, and 5% for investment banks in 2006 (CBB, 2006). The Arab banking system deals with most of the world currencies and the majority of banks in the Arab states open accounts for their customers in both local and foreign currencies such as in USD, and Euro. This is considered as an advantage compared to US banks which don't permit their customers to open accounts in any foreign currency. However, some of the Arab states may impose restrictions on holding foreign currencies accounts by their national residents.

Supervision on Arab banks: The banks facing various kinds of risks which may lead to financial crises. Examples of risks facing banking system are: operational risk including risk due to employees, due to process, due to system, and due to external factors such as external fraud and robberies, market risk including interest risk, currency and foreign exchange risk, holding equity risk, liquidity risk of shortage of cash to meet daily demand of funds, and credit risk which will increase the value of nonperforming loans and bad debt. Thus, there is a need to have a monitoring and controlling measures and efficient supervisory bodies. To cope with the issue, there are three levels of monitoring imposed on the bank activities; first at the national level which includes the central banks measures, the corporation laws requirements regarding disclosure requirements, and the capital market authority requirements. Second level is the regional level requirements, such as the supervision committee of Arab monetary fund. The third is the international level such as to accord with international regulatory organizations such as Basel I and II regulations, IASB standards and interpretations such as IAS 39. The applications of the above measures and regulations in the Arab banking system are between low and moderate, with exception of supervision imposed by the central banks, which is considered as restrictive measures compared to other measures. The majority of the Arab commercial banks adopted Basel I regulations regarding capital adequacy due to official decree published by Arab central banks or informally by issuing local regulations covering the majority of Basel I regulations, especially the capital adequacy. While, only few Arab central banks such as in Kuwait and Qatar were adopted Basel II regulations regarding management of operational risk, market discipline and transparency aspects.

Table 32. Types of banks as existed in the Arab economy in 2007

Classification	Types of banks	Existed in the Arab Economy
Ownership	Public 100% government	In five states
	Private	All Arab states
	Joint (Public and Private)	In some Arab states
	Cooperatives	In few Arab states
Fixed interest- profit	Conventional banks	All states except North Sudan
	Islamic banks	In 18 Arab states
Legal entity	Public corporations	All Arab states
	Private corporations	Few
	Credit union s	Not existed
	Postal saving banks	In few Arab sates
Purposes	Central Banks	All Arab states
	Commercial banks	All Arab states
	Development banks	Five Arab states
	Specialized banks	In the majority of Arab states
Major operations	Deposits- Loans	All Arab states
	Mortgage banks	Few
	Mutual saving banks	Not existed
	Loan Associations	Not existed
	Small micro credit banks	Few
Specialization	Universal banks	Not common
	General - commercial banks	All Arab states
	Industrial banks	Some Arab states
	Merchant banks	Not existed
	Housing and real estate banks	Some Arab states
	Agricultural banks	Some Arab states
Branches concept	Banks with branches	All Arab states
	Unit banking- one branch	Not existed
Nationality	National	All Arab states
	Foreign branches	In the majority of Arab states
	Offshore banks	Existed in few states such as in Bahrain

For example, the index of official bank supervisory power in Arab states ranged between 10 to 14, in which the point 14 presents the greater official supervisory powers exercised by government institutions including central banks, which means that the Arab banking system operates under strict supervision. In addition, the restrictions index for the Arab bank activities ranged between 7 to 12 points for the various Arab banks. The restriction on banking activity index ranged between 1 to 12 points as maximum, which means that there is relatively restrictive in terms of activities they allow to be conducted within the banking system such as dealing with securities and insurance activities, including Libya, Tunisia, and Lebanon which have index of over 8 points. The collateral percentage was 80% of granted loans by the Arab banks requiring collateral, which is higher than banking requirements in other regions. In addition, the bank regulatory capital to risk- weighted assets ranged between 10% and 20% for the individual Arab banks (IMF, 2007a, and World Bank, 2007c).

Performance of Arab banks: to measure the efficiency and the performance of the Arab banks, many measures and aspects may be examined including financial and quality measures. The financial measures include the profitability value and ratios, the size of deposits, the granted loans to deposit ratio, return on equity ratio, the return on total assets ratio, market share of the bank in the national economy, and the cost of implementing a specific service for a customer. The quality measures include customer satisfactions, use of ATM machines, and internet service, terms of granted loans, the time of completing a loan deal, number of current accounts opened to customers and other quality measures. For the accomplished profits. Table No. 33 indicates the net profits for the top ten Arab banks in the 2005 year. It shows that the top Arab bank which ranked number one in the Arab economy accomplished net profit of over $ 1.5 billion; the next two banks also accomplished a profit of over $ one billion. However, the next seven banks accomplished profits between a $ half billion and one billion in 2005, which is considered as a high record compared to the profit accomplished by other corporations operating in other sectors of the Arab economy.

To look for the banking system of each state, we find significant difference in the banking profitability as expressed by both return on equity and return on assets as presented in Table No. 34. It shows that the Arab states may be classified in three groups regarding the profitability of their banks. First; banks operating in Saudi Arabia accomplished the highest return as expressed by return on equity compared to other Arab states, with 75.3% followed by banks operated in Kuwait, and UAE which accomplished net profit ratio from 20.0% to 22%. The second group is about banks operated in Jordan and Lebanon which accomplished moderate income. The third group includes a low profit including banks work in Morocco and Tunisia with less than 10% of profit to equity. In addition, Jordan, Saudi Arabia, Kuwait and UAE have from 1.8% up to 4% of return on assets, while other states have less than 1% as indicated in the table.

Table 33. Top Arab Banks in 2005 based on accomplished net profit in $ million

Top Arab Banks	Rank in region	Net Profit in $ Million
Al-Rajahi Bank; SA	1	1502
National Commercial; SA	2	1366
SAMBA; SA	3	1072
Riyad Bank; SA	4	757
National bank; Kuwait	5	705
National Abu Dhabi; UAE	6	703
Saudi British; SA	7	668
Baanqu Saudi Fransi	8	591
Masherqbank; UAE	9	548
Abu Dhabi commercial	10	532
Arab bank; Jordan	11	503

Source: UAB (2006) United of Arab Bank Journal Issue 309; August, 2006; 275-280.

Table 34. Performance of Arab banking system in 2006

Arab states	Return on Equity	Return on Assets
Egypt	12.1%	0.7%
Jordan	20.6%	1.8%
Kuwait	21.6%	3.9%
Lebanon	11.9%	0.6%
Morocco	6.3%	0.5%
Saudi Arabia	75.3%	4.0%
Tunis	6.4%	0.5%
UAE	20.4%	2.5%

Source: IMF, 2006a and 2007a.

To consider the quality measures, it may be stated that the Arab banking system has witnessed a significant improvement due to the adoption of management and accounting information systems based on advanced software applications. In addition various reforms were occurred in the monetary and credit policies in the majority of Arab states, which reflected positively on banks operations. For example, Eltony (2003) reported that the implementation of financial reform leads to improvement in the Arab banking sectors for Arab countries such as Syria, Algeria and Yemen. However, the degree of efficiency of managing the Arab banks is different based on ownership, size, and legal entity bases. The perception in the Arab economy is that private banks are more efficient than public banks and foreign banks are more efficient than national banks.

This perception leads the Arab economy to go toward bank privatizations, permitting new licenses to private banks and opening of domestic banking system to foreign banks such that occurred in Algeria, in Syria and Tunisia between 1998 and 2005 (World Bank, 2006c). In addition to that, the perception of customers consider large banks more efficient than small banks, which have the ability to develop and adopt advanced accounting and management systems and have the ability to introduce the internet banking applications and other electronic applications. For example, Limam (2001) suggests that the efficiency and management of GCC banks can be improved by increasing bank size through resource consolidation, mergers and alliances with other banks.

Technology and Arab banks: the banking industry has witnessed a significant improvement in using new technology in computers and communications. The applications of both technologies in banking transactions produced a major improvement in accuracy, saving time and reducing cost of operation, more customers' satisfactions and more attractive services and new products and techniques. The new technology used by the banks may be classified into the following groups;

- Electronic fund transfer within the bank branches and between the worlds' banks.
- Internet banking service and applications.
- Telephone and mobile banking.
- ATMs services.
- Cards payment system including debt cards, credit cards, smart cards, point of sale cards, and magnetic cards.

The use of card payments system is increasing significantly in the Arab economy. For example, a survey showed an increase in the number of credit card holders and credit card accounts by 17.6% and 31.4% respectively in the Bahrain banking system during 2005 (CBB, 2006). The above new services create a burden on the Arab banks to adopt such services as well as may face the competition from foreign banks which now have the opportunity to access to national markets through cross- boarder services offered by internet transactions. Today, using of technology, internet services, ATMs and electronic transfers of funds is one of the indicators for measuring the performance and efficiency of banking system in the world economy.

However, the use of the above applications in the Arab economy is still limited under claims that the majority of the Arab customers do not trust internet or ATMs services. In addition, the World Bank report (2007c) indicated that the use of ATMs in Arab banks is still limited to 10 ATMs for each 100,000 inhabitants compared to 75 ATMs for banks working in the high income countries. It means that the percentage of ATMs uses is only 13 % of the uses of ATMs by banks located in the developed economies. The highest use of ATMs existed in banks working in Bahrain, Kuwait, Saudi Arabia and Lebanon, which have from 15 to 28 ATMs for each 100,000, while this number is much smaller in Egypt, Jordan and Palestine which have 10 ATMs per 100,000 or less.

The use of internet banking in Arab economies is also limited, and in case of its availability; a small share of customers is using such facility. This may be related to various causes such as the lack of customers' awareness, the lack of banking management awareness and support, security causes, and lack of infrastructures including software and hardware. For example, Rehman (2006) found that websites of most banks and financial companies in Kuwait were static and they had to take firm initiatives if they had to adopt e-commerce or electronic transactions. Jasimuddi (2001) reported that about 73% of the Saudi banks had a web presence, but only 25% of them were already offering full financial services over the Internet. Khalfan et al, (2006) found that the Arab Gulf banks have been slowing to launch e-banking services due to security and data confidentiality issues, lack of support from top management, customer insecurity, and lack of market-readiness. Yasin and Yavas (2007) found that some banks in Jordan offer Internet-based banking services, but they are rarely utilized as customers value prefer dealing with the bank's employees rather than using internet and they are concerned over security.

However, this is also applicable to electronic transfer of funds conducted by the banks. For example, there are two systems for electronic fund transfer between the world's banks to serve customers' needs. First one is the Federal Reserve Banks' Fed wire Funds Service known as Fedwire which works mainly to serve the American banks. The average daily value of transfers through Fedwire is approximately 2.3 trillion dollars with a half million payments and participations of about 7,500 depository institutions in 2005 (FEDWIRE, 2006). The second system is The Society for Worldwide Interbank Financial Telecommunication known as the SWIFT which serves all non American banks in the world. SWIFT is a cooperative organization registered in Belgian in 1973, and owned by its member banks of the world. The majority of international inter-bank messages use the SWIFT network which included about 8000 financial institutions in 205 countries; message traffic has grown seven-fold from 405 million messages in 1992 to nearly 2.9 billion messages in 2006. The volume of SWIFT transactions today is 11.4 million messages a day on average, the majority (55%) of such massages belong to transferring of payments, 36% for securities, 6.35% for treasury and 25% for other purposes (SWIFT, 2006). For Arab banks, using of electronic transferring funds through SWIFT system is still limited to 35 million massages, which formed only 1.2% of the world massages as presented in Table No. 35. It shows that the number of Arab members of SWIFT society is only 196 financial institutions which represent less than 40% of the total institutions working in the Arab economy. The connected firms to the system represent 6% of the total world connected firms. The Arab banks operating in UAE, Saudi Arabia, Egypt, Kuwait, Lebanon and Qatar represent the highest banks in dealing with electronic fund transfers, which has over two million received massages in 2006. While Banks working in Oman, Palestine, Sudan, Syria and Yemen, Libya, Iraq, Mauritania, and Djibouti represent the lowest rank in dealing with SWIFT system, which have less than one million massages in 2006 (SWAFT, 2006). However, electronic transferring through SWIFT are now under critical control from Arab central banks due to the exercised pressures by USA on Arab governments under what USA alleged about what called as "fighting terrorists and preventing money laundry". This pressure imposed by USA in Arab governments and other developing countries is extending even to European states as mentioned by the New York Times which revealed a secret undergoing US treasury program for terrorism investigations involving SWIFT transactions (SWIFT, 2006).

Major issues in the Arab banking sector: There are some issues attached to the banking system in the Arab economy such as; the low ratio of total deposits to the GDP, the high percentage of bounced checks in Arab banking system, the high percentage of bad loans known as nonperforming loans, the high margin between interest paid on deposits and interest earned on credit facilities, the low ratio of medium- long- term financing (more than one year) compared to short term loans, and the low ratio of leasing finance and the lack of credit financing offered by banks to some major economic sectors such as the agricultural sector, and the high ratio of loans granted to public sectors in some Arab states.

Table 35. Members' users and SWIFT traffic massages in the Arab banks during 2006

Arab states	SWIFT Members	Connected Firms	Sent in 1000	Received in 1000
United Arab Emirates	20	58	9,699	9,203
Saudi Arabia	13	20	9,853	2,615
Egypt	32	52	4,314	4,732
Kuwait	12	31	2,901	2,272
Lebanon	24	59	2,615	2,846
Qatar	8	19	2,459	2,211
Jordan	12	24	1,915	1,927
Tunisia	17	24	1,370	1,467
Algeria	6	23	1,122	1,414
Bahrain	11	62	1,940	1,726
Morocco	11	19	1,517	1,763
Oman	6	15	751	526
Palestine	2	10	147	573
Sudan	3	33	216	549
Syrian	3	8	211	398
Yemen	5	14	237	314
Libya	5	14	248	267
Iraq	3	13	54	79
Mauritania	2	11	32	63
Djibouti	1	3	38	45
Total Arab Banks	196	512	41,639	34,990
Total World Banks	2,301	8,105	2,864,540	2,864,540
Ratio to the world	8.5%	6.3%	1.5%	1.2%

Source: SWIFT, 2006.

In this section, we will discuss some of such issues existed in the Arab banking system and may be considered as disadvantages to this vital sector of the economy:

First: the increasing ratio of bad loans: The Arab banking system is suffering from high share of nonperforming loans to the total granted loans due to various reasons such as the weakness of the jurisdiction in the majority of Arab states, the shaky of collateral procedures, and due to the credit and banking culture in Arab environment. The average nonperforming loans in the Arab banking system were about 15%. It ranged between 25% in banking system in Egypt, and about 3% in banking system in Saudi Arabia as presented in Table No. 36. The nonperforming loans in Tunisia was 21% in 2006, in Lebanon was 16%, and in morocco 16% (IMF, 2007a). In addition, in other Arab banking systems not included in the table such as in Yemen for an example; the nonperforming loans form more than 30% (World Bank, 2007c). The main issue of nonperforming loans is the inefficient collateral systems existed in the Arab economy. The majority of collaterals for loans are against real estate and personal guarantees, with limited share for securities and financial collaterals. The liquidation of real estates to cover the nonperforming loans is a complex procedure in most of the Arab economy due to the weakness of jurisdiction system. The nonperforming loans lead to create allowances of uncollected loans according to generally accepted accounting principles, which will lead to reduce the annual profit of the bank.

Table 36. Nonperforming loans in the Arab banking system in 2005

	Nonperforming loans to total loans	Provisions to nonperforming loans
Egypt	25.0%	54.9%
Jordan	7.7%	57.8%
Kuwait	3.9%	100.6%
Lebanon	15.8%	
Morocco	15.7%	67.1%
Saudi Arabia	3.0%	164.0%
Tunis	20.9%	46.4%
UAE	6.9%	98.2%
Oman	7.8%	77.6%

Source: IMF, 2007a

For example, the deducted allowance for bad loans reached more than the accomplished profit for four banks, and increased the losses significantly for other six banks operating in Palestine as shown in the respected financial statements of the banks (Sabri, 2003a and 2003b). The nonperforming loans not only lead to decrease annual profit, but also lead the management of the bank to adopt more conservative policy of granting loans, which decrease the role of banking system in financing the private sector.

Second: the low percentage of deposits to GDP: The share of deposits to the GDP is one of the major indicators which measure the degree of saving in the national economy as well as to assess the efficiency of banking system in general. The banking deposits to the GDP ratio in the Arab economy is about 68% in

2005. It ranged between 14% in Sudan to 220% in Lebanon, in Jordan it was 123%, and in Palestine it was 90%, while in the rest of Arab states it was 80% or less (AMF, 2006b: Sabri, and Jaber, 2006). Considering the share of deposits to the GDP in the developed economies as well as in the middle income economies, it may be stated that the Arab banking system may recruit more savings, and even up to 50%, if better conditions are available regarding the customers' current saving and term- period deposits accounts, it will attract the deposits from foreign banks working in the Western world.

Third: Less access of private sector to the banking credit system: The share of public sector to the total credit granted by Arab banking system is high in some Arab states, which is considered a major disadvantage of banking system, because private sector may not compete with the state, leaving the private business in some economic sectors with less chance to be financed by the official banking sources. The average share of public credit to the total bank credit in Arab economy is 29% compared to 7% in developed economy and 20% to 25% in the middle income countries. However, the share of public credit in individual Arab states is much higher reaching 70% in Algeria, 45%in Yemen, 40% in Syria, 38% in Egypt, 50% in Lebanon and 48% in Qatar. This leads to the fact that the Arab business firm has 75% of sources of funds from owners' equity and retained earnings, 13% from other sources and only 12% from the banking system. In Egypt, the banking system offered only 10% as credit from the total sources of funds, and in Syria, the level of bank financing is less than 5% (AMF, 2006a; World Bank, 2006c; and World Bank, 2007c). In Palestine, the owners' equity is the major source of funds, followed by the credit offered by suppliers (accounts payable) which is considered as the second source of funds for most of the commercial, industrial, and agricultural institutions with an average of 10% of the total assets, while the role of other sources including microfinance system is confined to 10% of the total sources of funds available for business sector (Sabri, 2003a).

Fourth: the high margin between interest paid on deposits and interest earned on credit facilities. Due to the new policies adopted by some of the Arab central banks to leave the levels of interest rates for deposits and granted loans for the market and banks' decisions with minimum directions, we find that the majority of the Arab banks have high margin between debt and credit interests, which reach 100% or more. For example, the interest paid by Egyptian banks was 6.6% for deposits compared to 12.7% for short term loans as announced by the central bank of Egypt in May 2007 (CBE, 2006). In Lebanon, the interest paid by Lebanon banks for USD deposits was 4.2 % compared to 8.4% collected for granted loans in 2006 (BDL, 2006). In Qatar, the interest rate for deposits ranged between 3.6%

and 4.5%, while the interest rates stated for overdraft, bill discounts and short term loans was 7.6%, while the interest rate for loans up to three years was 9% and 18% for credit cards in 2006 (QCB, 2006). The Arab banks are justifying the high margin between debt and credit interest rates due to the high percentage of nonperforming loans and the required ratios of deposits to be hold by central banks.

Chapter 5

ARAB DEVELOPMENT FUNDS

The Second important financial institutions existed in the Arab economy is the Arab development funds. The concept behind establishing the Arab development funds was related to enhancing Arab unity, developing integration of Arab economy and encouraging joint development projects as stated in the objectives of such funds. The first Arab development fund was established and owned by government of Kuwait in 1961, followed by other ten funds established in the seventies as a result of significant increase in oil prices occurred at that decade. Later on, in the eighties; two specialized Arab funds were established in Dubai and Riyadh.

The main aim of the Arab development funds is to grant loans for government developing projects concentrated in the Arab economy as well as in non-Arab states. The Arab development funds mainly deal with government projects and in few cases they may deal with private sector. The granted loans offered by the Arab development fund are classified as Official Development Assistance (ODA) which is defined as loans granted in concessional financial terms which contains at least 25% grant element or above. The grant element may be measured by stating the difference between the granted loan by the development fund and the commercial loan granted by a commercial bank considering the following factors:

- Interest rates and the way of calculating it, whether on the remaining balance or the whole amount.
- Administrative fees, and other premium cost
- The grace period for the loan.
- The repayments schedule and periods.
- The guarantee and collateral terms.

- Repayment of the principal of the loan terms.
- Some ODA loans include a grant which covers a percentage of the loan.
- Other conditions attached to the loan.

The Arab development funds account for thirteen funds including national funds and regional funds as shown in Table No. 37, the national funds are; the Kuwait fund, the Libyan Arab foreign company, Abu Dhabi fund, the Iraq fund, and Saudi fund.

Table 37. Arab development funds and their owners' equities (Capital and reserves) in 2005

Funds	Location	Established	Equities $ Million
National Funds			
Kuwaiti Fund for Arab economic Development	Kuwait	1961	12,566
Saudi Fund for Development	Riyadh	1974	8,265
Iraq Fund for external development (data for 2001)	Baghdad	1977	1,896
Abu Dhabi Fund for Arab Economic Development (data for 2003)	Abu Dhabi	1971	1,034
Libyan Arab Foreign Investment Company	Tripoli	1972	887
Regional Funds			
Arab Fund for Economic and Social Development (	Kuwait	1973	7,768
BADEA	Khartoum	1973	2,825
Inter-Arab Investment Guarantee Corporation	Kuwait	1974	287
OPEC Special fund for International Development	Vienna	1975	4,907
Arab Monetary Fund (AMF)	Abu Dhabi	1975	3,487
Islamic Development bank (IDB)	Jeddah	1975	7,976
AGFUND	Riyadh	1981	270
The Arab Trade Financing Program	Abu Dhabi	1989	751
Total Equity of Arab funds (paid capital and accumulated reserves)			52,871

Source: The annual reports (2005- 2006) for the above development funds.

The net equities of the Arab national funds ranged between $ 12.5 billion for Kuwait fund, $ 8.3 billion to Saudi fund $ 1.9 billion to Iraq fund, and the rest national funds have $ 1 billion equity or less, the Arab national funds owned fully by their respective governments. While the Arab regional funds have equities ranged between $ 8 billion for Islamic development bank, to $ 7.7 billion for the AFESD fund to $ 4.9 billion for OPEC fund as indicated in their financial statements and annual reports. The total equity (paid capital and accumulated reserves) of Arab funds was about $ 53 billion in 2005, which is a large pool of funds, it is equivalent to 58% of the total of equities for all Arab commercial and Islamic banks working in the Arab economy; thus may be used to lead the development and prosperity of the region, mainly in Arab and Islamic countries. All of the Regional development banks are owned fully by Arab states with exception of Islamic Development Bank and OPEC fund. The Islamic development banks owned by 56 Islamic states, but the Arab states represent the majority of ownership of the bank, the OPEC owned by the OPEC members, but also Arab OPEC members own the majority of the ownership of the fund. These funds offered long and short term loans, grants, and technical assistance. The majority of Arab Development Funds (8 out of 13), including Islamic Development Bank, the OPEC, Arab Fund for Economic and Social Development ABEDA, AGFUND, Abu Dhabi Fund, Saudi Fund for Development and Kuwait Fund for Arab Development established a coordinating group since 1974 and up to now, whose purpose is to organize their operations known as the coordination Group of Arab National and Regional Development Institutions (ANRDI, 2004).

The main objectives for these funds can be summarized as follows as stated in their annual reports and their establishments' laws and bylaws (Sabri, 1997, and annual reports of the listed funds, 2006):

1. Arab Monetary Fund; granting loans to support balance of payment of Arab States.
2. Arab Fund for Economic and Social Development; to grant loans based on concessional terms to participate in financing economic projects in Arab States.
3. Arab Bank for Economic Development in Africa (BADEA); granting loans of concessional terms for African projects, and to offer technical assistance for African states.
4. The Inter- Arab Investment Guarantee Corporation; offering guarantee of investment in Arab States and to support exporting in Arab State.
5. Arab Gulf Program for United Nations Development Organizations (AGFUND); supporting sustainable human development efforts and target the neediest groups in the developing countries, particularly women and children.
6. Arab Trade Financing Program (ATFP); to enhance trading among Arab states and to finance intra- Arab trading.
7. Islamic Development Bank; financing of trading, Leasing, forward selling and offer free interest loans.

8. OPEC: Special Fund for International Development; to offer loans for projects of concessional terms for developing countries and loans to support balance of payment of developing states.

9. Abu Dhabi Fund for Arab Economic Development; to offer loans for projects in Arab and developing countries of concessional terms, to sharing in equities of corporations located in Arab and non-Arab States and to supervising and conducting the loans granted by UAE government.

10. Kuwaiti Fund for Arab Economic Development: to offer Loans of concessional terms for Arab projects and others

11. Saudi Fund for Development; to offer loans for projects of concessional terms and to share in equity of corporations in Arab and non-Arab States

12. Iraq Fund for external Development; to offer loans for Arab projects of concessional terms.

13. Libyan Arab Foreign Investment Company; to offer loans for economic projects of concessional terms in Arab and non-Arab states and to share in equities of business corporations.

Most of the Arab funds are concentrated in financing public and government projects rather than private projects, in spite of some Arab funds that may deal directly with private sector. In addition, they target specific sectors such as transportation, which has a share of 26.7% of the total allocated funds, the energy projects 18.6%, and the agriculture and agro-industry 15.1%. The definition of Arab funds come from the fact the Arab states own fully or the majority of the capital such in case of OPEC, Islamic Development Bank. However, in spite of the fact that all mentioned Arab funds are owned fully or partially (majority) by Arab governments, they offered loans, aids and other services to the majority of the developing countries. The beneficiaries that deal with Arab development funds have increased and extended to almost all developing countries. However, there are only two Arab funds which are dealing exclusively with Arab states, including the Arab Monetary Fund and the Arab Funds for Economic and Social Development. While the other funds offered loans to countries in Africa, Asia, Latin American and in few cases in Europe. The share of Arab economy from the Arab funds ranged from 100% by the AFESD, and AMF, to 54% by Kuwaiti fund, 79% by Abu Dhabi fund, 49% by Islamic Development Bank and Saudi fund.

However, this share is very low which was 17% of the total appropriations of OPEC which were allocated to Arab economy, in spite of the fact that the Arab governments owned the majority of the OPEC fund capital, while the BADEA fund allocating their grants and loans to non-Arab African countries. Finally, the average of allocated funds for Arab economy paid by Arab funds was 61% of the total granted loans and grants in 2005 as shown in Table No. 38.

The main contribution of loans and grants come from Islamic Development Bank with 28% share, followed by AFESD with 22.4% share, followed by Kuwait fund with a share of 18%. While the other funds contributed of less than 8% for each. The share of loans granted by the Arab development funds for African states from was about 14.6%, while it was 22% for Asian states, and 2.1% to other states (AMF, 2006a).

Table 38. Accumulated operations for Arab development funds in $ Million up to 2005

Funds	Accumulated operation	Share to total	Projects in Arab states	Ownership of Arabs
Kuwaiti Fund for Arab economic Development	13,784.8	18.0%	54%	100%
Islamic Development bank (IDB)	21,438.4	28.1%	49%	75%**
Saudi Fund for Development	7,831.2	7.7%	49%	100%
Arab Fund for Economic and Social Development (AFESD)	17,070.8	22.4%	100%	100%
OPEC Special Fund for International Development	5,872.2	7.7%	17%	62%**
Arab Monetary Fund (AMF)	4,440.0	5.8%	100%	100%
Arab Bank for Economic Development in Africa(BADEA)	2,494.8	3.3%	1%	100%
Abu Dhabi Fund for Arab Economic Development	3,421.6	4.5%	79%	100%
Iraq Fund for external development	1,733*	2.5%		100%
Total operations up to 2005	76,353.8	100%	61%	100%

Sources: AFM, 2006a; * OPEC, 2002, up to end of 2001; ** Sabri, 1997.

Evaluating the performance of the Arab development funds in the last three decades is a difficult task, especially when we want to examine their role in enhancing the Arab economy. However it is clear that about $ 50 billion were allocated to developed projects in the Arab economy, but the output of such funds is limited compared to what is available as expressed by the total capital and accumulated reserves. Accordingly, the following section is devoted to examine the performance of the Arab development funds, which will include the major issues facing their roles in enhancing the Arab economy and prosperity based on analysis of the financial data of such development bank funds and other economic measures (Sabri, 1997).

First: The majority of Arab developed funds' assets are invested in deposits with local and foreign commercial and central banks, in bonds, in securities in foreign and Arab economies. Thus, the invested share in developing the Arab economic projects is still at low level considering the stated objectives of such funds. The outstanding loans for all funds are limited to one third of their total assets. Nevertheless many studies argue that the Arab funds operations are not sufficient compared to the available sources for those funds and to the total funds allocated to the invested economic developments in the recipients from all sources. This situation is justified that funds' management has to guarantee its continuity of work, in maintaining profitable and secured investment. In addition, there is a need to produce the necessary revenues to cover their operational expenditures, which may not be covered by the limited income generated from loans granted on concessional terms to the region.

Second: There are large amounts of uncalled capital shares for the existing Arab funds which may be added to the present capital and reserves, which may improve the available sources of funds. The majority of Arab development funds have a high authorized capital values compared to the actual paid capital. This includes Islamic Development Bank; the Arab Fund for Economic and Social Development, the Arab Monetary Fund, the OPEC Special Fund for International Development, the Kuwaiti Fund for Arab economic Development, the Iraqi fund for external Development, and the Arab Bank for Economic Development in Africa. The uncalled capital of Arab funds is more than $ 6 billion.

Third: The Arab funds depend exclusively on their capital and reserves in financing their operations. None of the Arab funds uses external financial sources to extend their funding resources. Only the Islamic Development Bank issued Islamic bonds to finance specific projects in 2005-2006.This situation limits the activities of funds' operations to the minimum level. These funds suppose to work through their capital as well as other collected funds from various sources as stated in most of their bylaws. The fund mechanism is generally built on the idea that to work as finance pool which collect from all sources of funds besides the capital and reserves. The average debt to equity ratio of Arab Development funds is about 10% compared to 81% for the World Bank which rank number one in the world economy as development bank, and 94% for Arab commercial banks.

Fourth: The activity ratio: the activity ratio for the Arab funds which measures the ratio between the accumulated financial operations to owners' equity ranged between less than 1.5 to 3 times, with an average of 2.25 times. This ratio is at low level compared to the activity ratio of the world and the regional development fund as well as compared to Arab commercial banks. For example, the activity ratio of the World Bank is ten times, which means that the World Bank owners' equity value has been rotated for ten times over the 50 years of its operation.

Fifth: High percent of the non used approved loans: The non used approved loans ratio forms a significant part of the total committed loans granted by the Arab funds, which is higher than the acceptable limit. The delay of withdrawal of the committed amounts as scheduled for payments is related to either the funds and/ or to the recipients. The non-used granted loans are measured by the dispensed to committed loans ratio. The ratio for the Arab funds is varying from one fund to another and from one operation to another, but on average, it was about 68%, which means that the non-used loans ratio was 32% for Arab Funds as shown in Table No 39. The Dispensed to committed loans ratio was 62% for AFESD fund, which represents unused loans over $ 6 billion and 65% for BADEA which presents unused loans over $ 668 million in 2005, according to their annual report compared to 95% to the IMF, and 75% for the World Bank (World Bank, 2006b). However, an average fair ratio of 20% discrepancy between the disbursed and the committed loans may be acceptable due to the nature of preparing and implementing the majority of the long- term projects. Some funds have high ratios of non- disbursements loans for various reasons related to the type of the project, the management of the fund or for the conditions of the recipient country.

Sixth: Financial performance of the Arab development funds: The net profit ratio of the Arab development funds is expected to be high as long as the majority of their assets are invested in deposit accounts, bonds, securities and sharing in equities of corporations, and only one third are allocated for granting loans in concessional terms. Nevertheless, the average net profit ratio of the Arab funds is low of about 4% compared to 15% for a commercial bank. The net profit value for Islamic development bank was $ 339 million for AFESD, $ 158 million for BADEA, and $ 209 million for IDB, and in 2005, which presents a net profit ratio to owners' equity of 4.4%, 5.6 %, and 3.1% respectively for the three Arab development funds.

Seventh: Loan terms and the grant element: All Arab funds grant loans for development projects, which may be classified as Official Development Assistance (ODA). The interest rate of Arab funds ranged between 0.5% and 7%, the lowest rate is charged by the IDB, and the Kuwaiti Fund, while the highest rate charged by the Arab Monetary Fund in case of compensatory and contingency loans, as presented. The grace period of loans granted by the Arab funds ranged between 2 to 10 years, with an average of about 5 years. The repayments period ranged between 5 years and 25 years maximum, except for AMF, which has a maximum of 7 years. The above conditions produce a grant element of an average 42% of the total loans. However, the grant element ratio differs from one Arab development fund to another and from one loan to another.

Table 39. Financial indicators of selected Arab development funds
2005- 2006 in $ million

Major Financial Items	AFESD	BADEA	IDB
Cumulative Loan Commitments	16,845	2,235	3,990
Balance of outstanding granted Loans*	6,313	653	3,388
Cumulative Loan Disbursements	10,743	1,567	2,490
Cumulative Loan Repayments	4,260	866	2,150
Net Profit for the year 2005	339	158	209
Net Profit to equity ratio	4.4%	5.6%	3.1%
Total Assets	7,955	3,121	8,520
% of disbursements to committed loans	62%	65%	56%
* Islamic operations for IBD			

Sources: The AFESD 2005; BADEA, 2005, and IDB, 2006.

Eight: Restrictions on granting loans: There are various restrictions and limitations imposed by the foundation agreements of the Arab funds. Such restrictions are considered as obstacles in enhancing the role of the Arab funds in developing the region. These limitations are related to maximum limits on granted loans for a project and for one state as well as other conditions, which can be summarized as follow:

- The Maximum Participation of a single project as a percentage of the total cost which are stated by the Arab Bank for Economic Development in Africa, Arab Fund For Economic and Social Development, Kuwaiti Fund for Arab Economic Development, Abu Dhabi Fund for Arab Economic Development, Saudi Fund for Development.

- The accumulated outstanding loans for a country should not exceed a percentage of the fund's capital or owners' equity.
- The total outstanding loans or financing operations should not exceed a percentage of total owners' equity as stated by Islamic Development Bank. Abu Dhabi Fund for Arab Economic Development and Saudi Fund for Development.
- Borrowers from AMF should offer reforming economic plans as stated by Arab Monetary Fund.

Chapter 6

ARAB INSURANCE COMPANIES

The insurance sector is witnessing a significant development in Arab economy but it is still considered less important than the banking sector. The Insurance sector in Arab economy is an old sector; some insurance corporations were established between1900 and 1935 such as the Ahlia, and Al-Sharq corporations in Egypt. The majority of the insurance firms is working as a private sector with exception in Iraq, Syria and Egypt. In Egypt now; both public and private insurance corporations exist. The majority of insurance corporations exist in Arab economy are national corporations, with some foreign life and general insurance corporations such as the American ALICO which deals in life insurance in Lebanon and Jordan, and AXA Assurance of France, and Zurich Insurance in Morocco. Today, there are about 276 insurance and reinsurance corporations working in the Arab states in 2007. The majority of such corporations exist in Lebanon, Jordan, AUE, Egypt, Saudi Arabia, and Tunis. Other Arab countries have less than 15 insurance corporations for each (GAIF, 2007). The Arab insurance sector is considered as the second important sector regarding employment opportunities, after banks among the financial institutions. For example, in Egypt the insurance sector hires about 15,000 employees in 2003 (AIM, 2006). The insurance business in the Arab economy may be classified into three groups; such as general insurance group including casualty and property insurance, the life insurance group, and the reinsurance group for the first two groups.

The Arab insurance business firm may be organized either in public or private corporations, or in a cooperative firm according to the related laws, but it is not possible to work as a sole firm or as a partnership firm. The Arab insurance business is working within the framework of the related laws and regulations including corporate laws, cooperative laws, the insurance laws, and under the supervision of the supervisory government agencies. The used name for the supervisory government agency is different from one Arab state to another such as Jordanian Insurance commission, the Egyptian Insurance supervisory Authority, Kuwaiti Insurance department, and the Qatari Insurance supervisor. The existing Arab insurance firms may work in one group or two groups or in the three groups together. The majority of Arab insurance corporations work mainly in one of the three groups. However, various insurance corporations deal with two groups of activities such as with life and general insurance simultaneously, or in case of three groups' activities, the insurance corporation deals with life insurance, general insurance and reinsurance activities concurrently. The firm deals with more one group of activities should have independent management and financial systems for each group of the insurance activities. There are other types of insurance such as Islamic insurance corporations, cooperative insurance, and special insurance funds. In the following section, more details about the major groups of the insurance sector in the Arab economy will be presented; while later on will explore the Islamic insurance company known as Takaful firm.

First group: is related to casualty and property insurance, and is known as general insurance, to be distinguished from the life group of insurance. This group includes personal and property auto insurance , casualty insurance, health insurance, liability insurance, travel insurance, insurance against fire, earthquakes insurance, workmen's accidents insurance, insurance against theft, medical and health insurance, engineering insurance, insurance to protect agriculture losses and many other types of insurance. However, the health and medical insurance may be considered one part of life group of insurance. The existence, size, and types of general insurance vary from one Arab state to another, and it is mainly based on whether a specific type of insurance is voluntary or compulsory. The most important sector among insurance activities is the obligatory insurances. For example, in Palestine Out of the total, 74% of the value of insurance premium comes from car accident insurance which is obligatory, while other types of insurances are voluntary, have less share compared to the total insurance business, such as health insurance, which had 5%, insurance against fire 4%, maritime insurance 6%, life insurance 5% and other types of insurance 6%. Among the above types of insurance, the maritime insurance is considered as the most profitable activity based on the financial statements of the Palestinian insurance companies (Sabri, 2003a and Sabri, 2003b). In Egypt also, we found that about 78% of net operation comes from car accidents compared to other types of general accidents (AIM, 2006). This is also applied to general insurance in Morocco, in which car insurance forms more than 50% of non life insurance as shown in the annual reports of Morocco insurance corporations.

Second group: It is related to life insurance that provides protection against financial loss that may happen as a result of the death of a family spouse which leads to risk the family loosing its income suddenly. The life insurance may be presented in various programs, which may be connected to saving and retirements programs or to health treatment, or may be concentrated in a specific age group connected with education or other purposes. The life insurance activity is still premature in most of Arab countries and has a minor role in the Arab financial sector, even in some countries such as Egypt, which working in Life insurance in more than one century. The share of life insurance to total insurance in the Arab economy was about 17%, comparing to 83% to the property and casualty Insurance group in 2004. The highest share of life insurance may be found in Egypt, Lebanon and Morocco, while the less share of life insurance found in Saudi Arabia, Algeria and Qatar. In general, the life insurance in Arab economy is still very limited compared to some developed countries such as Japan and Netherlands, in which the share of life insurance exceeds the share of all other types of insurances (III, 2007). In addition, the life insurance sector amounts to only $ 17 premium per capita for the Arab citizen, which is about 14 percent of GDP compared to $ 1300 premium per capita for high income countries (World Bank, 2006c). This issue may has several reasons related to the religion and cultural causes, or to the instability of the political situation, since life insurance means payments from customers for a long time period, before the possibility of his family to get any returns. The third reason is related to the weakness and small capital of Arab insurance working in life insurance compared to the respective firms working in the Western world. Moreover, life insurance is hard to sell in the Arab business environment.

Third group: The third group is related to re-insurance activities: The insurance corporations supposed to reinsure issued policies in other national or international reinsurance corporations, especially in case of some types of insurance, and based on the value of the insurance premiums and the expected total compensation, in order to share in paying compensation in case of costly insurance accidents. The reinsurance corporations is supposed to work with relatively high capital to absorb expected losses. Thus to deal with this issue, there were various joint projects to establish joint reinsurance companies to work in the Arab economy. There are two examples; first is the Arab Reinsurance Corporation which was established in 1972 in Beirut, to carry out the reinsurance needs of Arab Insurance companies. It is owned by Arab states, mainly Saudi Arabia, 14%, Egypt 13%, Libya 12%, Lebanon 12% and Syria11% and 38 % for other Arab states. The total assets were about $ 101 million with accumulated capital of $50 million according to its annual report in 2005. The second joint project was the establishment of the Arab Insurance Group (ARIG) as a Bahraini Shareholding Company in 1980 by the United Arab Emirates, Kuwait and Libya. It works in general causality and life insurance and reinsurance, but it is mainly aimed to work in reinsurance business, the total assets was of ARIG was $ 929 million with owners' equity of $ 293 in 2006. However, the annual net written premiums for the top Arab reinsurance companies is still modest compared to the world top reinsurance companies such as Munich Re ($ 21.2 billion), Swiss Re ($ 21.2 billion), Berkshire Hathaway of US ($ 10.1 billion), Hannover Re of US ($ 2.7 billion) and Lloyd's of UK ($ 6.7 billion) in 2005 (RIM, 2006).

Finally, we can point out various issues and problems regarding the low performance of the insurance sector in the Arab economy as presented below:

Table 40. Summary of the Arab insurance corporations

Arab States	No. of firms	Direct premium written 2004 In $ million		Leading Firms	
		Life insurance	Non- Life insurance	Life insurance	Non- Life insurance
Algeria	9	26	454	SAA	SAA
Oman	5	38	236	National	
Egypt	19	211	400	Misr	Misr
Kuwait	13	95	393	Gulf	Kuwait
Jordan	29	32	251	ALICO	Middle East
Lebanon	50	180	397	ALICO	Medgulf
Morocco	10	323	1,049	RMA	RMA
Qatar	8	12	271		Qatar Insurance
Saudi Arabia	18	50	1,146		
Tunisia	15	43	511	STAR	HAYETT
UAE	27	245	1,239	Abu Dhabi	Dubai
Syria	9				
Libya	6				
Palestine	9				
Sudan	13				
Total		1.3 billion	7.6 billion		
Compared to					
USA	..	495 billion	603 billion		
Japan		389 billion	106 billion		
Netherlands		32 billion	27 billion		

Sources: III, 2007 and GAIF, 2007.

First: The Arab insurance sector failed to act as a saving vehicle in the Arab economy, especially, when we see the immaterial annual collected gross premium which was about $ 1.5 billion in all Arab states in 2004, compared to $ 495 billion in USA, $398 in Japan, and $ 32 billion in Netherlands as shown in Table 40. The life insurance gross premium ranged from $ 12 million in Qatar to $ 323 million in Morocco. The highest collected annual premium was in Morocco, Egypt and Lebanon in 2004 (III, 2007). The collected annual premium may cover compensations and administration cost, while almost nothing remains to be invested in the Arab economy. The life insurance firm in many economies is considered as the most attractive saving instrument; thus as a pool for investment in various economic sector, a role which is completely absent in case of Arab insurance sector.

Second: The general insurance businesses is much better that the life insurance, but still is limited compared to developed economies. For example, the direct premium collections for all types of general insurance was about $7,6 billon for the majority of Arab states compared to $ 603 billion in USA, and $ 106 billion in Japan and $ 27 billion in Netherlands as an example. The most important general insurance sector exist in Saudi Arabia, AUE, and Morocco, which have annual premium over one $ one billion for each.

Third: The tiny disadvantage in the insurance business is also applied for the insurance firms working in this sector. For example, the majority of the Arab insurance firms is working within small capital ranged between $ 3 million to $50 million with an average of $ 15 million per company, with a minimum capital of $ 2 million for the Majority of the Arab states. Accordingly, we find the highest value of the anural gross direct insurance premiums ranged between $ 8 million to $ 87 million in case of RMA (Royale Marocaine d'Assurance) of Morocco as the top Arab life insurance working in Arab economy regarding the life insurance, and ranged from $ 16 million to $ 518 million in case of Dubai insurance company regarding the general insurance premium. By comparing that to the top world insurance corporation, we'll find how much this sector is tiny compared to the world economy. For example, the Allianz insurance company of Germany and the American international Group which ranked as the top world insurance companies have annual revenues of over $ 100 billion for each in general insurance sector in 2004. While ING of Netherlands and AXA of France in 2004 accomplished over $ 130 billion annually in life and health insurance sector (III, 2007).

Fourth: Reinsurance issue: The insurance corporations are supposed to reinsure issued policies in international or national reinsurance corporations, especially in case of some types of insurance, and based on the value of the insurance premium and total compensation. In order to share in compensation payments in case of costly insurance accidents. However, there is no enough supervision on this issue regarding the details of agreements, the class of the reinsured company, and the percentage of the reinsured amount. However, the majority of Arab Insurance Corporations deal with the international reinsurance firms such as the Munich reinsurance in Germany, and Swiss reinsurance in Switzerland. While the two major Arab reinsurance corporations and other Arab reinsurance corporations still have limited share in this market.

Fifth: The commitment of insurance companies towards their clients regarding paying compensation without complex procedures is considered as a major issue in the Arab insurance business, due to the weakness of the legal system in the Arab states. Thus, the insurance companies may not meet their commitments as should be, accordingly, a substantial part of insurance cases end in courts taking a long time to be solved or agreed upon.

The last issue is about the role of the Arab insurance sector in encouraging the foreign direct investment; due to the absence of special insurance programs such as insurance on political risk. In addition, a mature business insurance system will serve foreign enterprises against various possible risks which keep the conditions of the Arab business environment as attractive as possible.

Chapter 7

ISLAMIC FINANCE AND INSTITUTIONS

After four decades of emerging what is known as Islamic finance, it may be stated that, today we have materialized Islamic financial sector, which includes mainly four significant types of financial institutions and securities, which now existed in the Arab economy as presented in Table No, 41. The Islamic bank, which were started as early in the sixties and the seventies with few banks located in Egypt, Jordan and Arab Gulf as the first Islamic financial vehicle. Today, we have about 100 Islamic banks existed in about 19 Arab states. They are operating mainly in Bahrain 27, Saudi Arabia 10, Egypt 8, Sudan 9, and UAE 9, while other Arab states have from one to five Islamic banks (IIBI, 2007). In addition, there is a new bank in the way of operating in Syria. One decade later, another financial Islamic vehicle was evolved known as Takaful, which was, started operation as an insurance cooperative firm, mainly in Sudan and Arab Gulf, and then it was extended to other Arab countries such as in Jordan and Tunisia. In addition, it is now some Islamic insurance corporations under establishment in Syria and Palestine. In 2007, there are about 23 Takaful firms working in Arab economy as cooperatives or in a base of other legal firms. The Saudi Arabia has the largest number of Takaful firms, which reached 12 insurance firms in 2007, followed by Bahrain, Sudan, Qatar, Tunisia and Jordan respectively. The third Islamic vehicle evolved around 1995, and became known as the Islamic investment fund, which is managed mostly by Islamic and non-Islamic banks. It includes various types of funds such as equity funds, Ijarah fund related to leasing activities, bond fund, balanced and hybrid fund and real state fund. The fourth part of Islamic finance is related to a new financial instrument, which is considered one part of traditional marketable securities. This new financial Islamic security includes sovereign bonds, Sukuks, Ijarah security, and corporate bond security.

These securities are traded in the last few years as in the case of Islamic investment funds in the Arab Gulf states, and mainly in Qatar and Bahrain.

Table 41. Summary of Islamic finance as existed in the Arab economy in 2007

Islamic Finance	Number Existed in 2007	Arab States
1. Islamic banks	100 banks	Existed in 19 Arab states
2. Takaful (insurance)	22 Insurance firms	Saudi Arabia, Bahrain, Sudan, Qatar, Tunisia, and Jordan
3: Islamic investment funds	113 funds	Saudi Arabia, UAE, Kuwait, Bahrain; and Qatar
4: Islamic Securities	Murabaha equity security	Bahrain, Qatar,
	Sovereign Sukuks- short term	Bahrain
	Sovereign Sukuks long term	Bahrain, Qatar,
	Islamic corporate bonds	limited in number Saudi corporations
	Ijara leasing security	Bahrain, Qatar,

Sources: compiled by the author based on: IIBI (2007) Institute of Islamic Banking and Insurance http://www.islamic-banking.com and FII: Filaka International (2007); available on line: www.filaka.com

This section will be devoted to discuss the above four instruments of Islamic finance as existed in the Arab economy as presented below. However, the Islamic banks, Islamic insurance, investment funds and Islamic securities also exist in Islamic Asian states and extend to some European states and Northern America, but this book deals only with Islamic finance experience in the Arab economy.

First: Islamic Banks: The Islamic bank is operated based on Islamic legislations as well as governmental monetary regulatory rules and regulations. The concept of profit in Islam is based on trading activities and the prohibition of usury. Thus; investing money should be considered as one factor which may not produce a return without the risk of being invested and a loss or profit may be produced. An Islamic bank was first vehicle to be emerged as a part of what now so called Islamic finance. It aims to maximize social and economic return to the whole society as well as to the concerned parties including stockholders and investors as depositors. The sources of funds of the Islamic bank are the equities and deposits; Islamic banks do not use debt as a source of financing, either from depositors or from other financial institutions or issuing corporate bonds, but may issue what is known as Islamic bonds (Sukuk), however, this choice is not exercised by commercial Islamic banks, but rather used by the development Islamic bank (DIB). The Islamic bank operates as a conventional bank, but it does deal with interest, which creates major differences between Islamic and business banks in terms of philosophy, functions, services, and sources and uses of funds, thus; lead to different economic role, and targeted customers. Islamic banks can grant interest-free loans to the poor and the needy and students. They may invest in common stocks only, while business banks can invest in different kinds of securities. However, the Islamic banks offered most of the banking services which are offered by conventional banks with some exceptions as indicated in Table No. 42.

Table 42. Similarities and differences between Islamic and conventional banks

Banking activities	Conventional Bank	Islamic banks
I: Sources of funds		
Capital and R.E.	Yes	Yes
Deposits; (fixed interest)	Yes	Yes (participating in profit)
Loans and bonds	Yes	No
II: Use of funds		
Investment in loans	Yes	No
Investment in securities	Yes	Yes (no fixed interest securities)
Participation in business	Small	Yes (main field of investment)
Investment in foreign currencies	Yes	Yes
III: Services rendered		
Current accounts	Yes	Yes
Credit card	Yes	Yes; no overdraft
Letters of guarantees	Yes	Yes
Bills discounted	Yes	No
Forward rate and arbitrage	Yes	No
Pre- arranged profit basis	No	Yes
Letter of credit	Yes	Yes (100% down payment)
Credit cards	Yes	Yes with no over-draft
Forward rate and arbitrage	Yes	No
Underwriting in securities	Yes	Equities and Islamic instruments
IV: Cost of Capital		
Expected return on capital	Yes	Yes (stockholders)
Expected return on bonds	Yes	Yes Sukuk and Islamic bonds
Expected return on deposits	No	Yes

Source: Sabri and Jaber, 1985 and 1987.

As shown in the table, the major differences are existed in the major uses of funds, while the Islamic bank participates in various investment projects, the major operations of Islamic banks include: Murabaha, Mutajra, Istisna'a and installment sale and other legitimate project investment, joint ventures known as Musharakah accords with Islamic Shariah compatible. Murabaha means that a sales process of commodity is based on cost plus margin of profit. Istisna'a means joint projects including financing of manufacturing of goods and equipment, and construction works. Establishing and participating in projects are the main investment areas for Islamic banks since clients ask the bank to participate in their own activities, and the bank becomes a partner which bears the risk as the client on a proportionate basis. The conventional bank main use of fund is granting loans using different instruments of lending. Depositors in Islamic banks are risk takers; they participate in profits of the bank as pre-agreed, but they have priority over the assets of the bank in case of liquidation (Sabri and Jabr, 1985, and 1987). However, the importance of each type of Islamic bank operations and services are different from one service and function to another, and from one bank to another. For example, the Al-Rajhi Bank which ranks number one among Islamic banks got the main revenues from installment sale of 69% of the total bank revenue, 23% from the Mutajra operation, 4% from Istisna'a and 3% from Murabaha, and 1% from other transactions in 2006 (Al-Rajhi, 2006). To examine small Islamic bank revenue, we find that 57% of total revenues came from Murabaha, 28% form trading in currencies, 9% from banking services, 2% from trading in real estate, and 4% from other revenues as reported by the Islamic Arab Bank of Palestine (IAB, 2006).

The Islamic bank should hold different accounting records such as having separate accounts for each type of investment, projects, securities portfolio, and joint projects with customers. In addition, special reserves for risks should be hold, due to the difficulty of measuring net profit of long-term projects on annual basis. This reserve may be called "reserve for investment risk". And to have a special account to represent the social role of Islamic banks regarding the Zakat fund which includes collected Zuka from depositors as well as from shareholders and the bank itself. Finally, a systematic way should be developed and adopted concerning the distribution of profits over the various types of depositors including depositors for specific projects, for specific term, depositors for non-specific projects, saving accounts holders and current accounts holders. Islamic banks operations are conducted under supervision of central banks, corporate laws, capital market authorities, as well as under a Shariah advisory council which authorized activities of the bank, and permits transactions if they comply with Shariah principles. In addition, it also has to adopt international control standards such as Basel I and II regulations concerning adequacy of capital and measuring the bank operations risk as well as the international generally accepted accounting principles and disclosures requirements as applied to the conventional banks.

After four decades of Islamic banking experience, it may conclude that this vehicle of financial institutions is still not completed, to be judged compared to traditional banks. Even the majority of Islamic banks operating in the Arab economy are listed in the Arab stock exchanges. The success of such banks is varied as expressed by their owners' equity, total value of collected deposits, total assets and annual net income. There are many small Islamic banks facing real problems in collecting deposits and in covering their annual operating cost due to weak performance of bank assets. While on the other side, we find about nine Arab Islamic banks managed to be in the list of the top 100 Arab banks in 2005 among both conventional and Islamic banks as expressed by total assets, credits and equities. Such leading Islamic banks are considered as successful stories in the Islamic finance, accomplished ranks of 5, 17, 26, and 44 among the first fifty top Arab banks. The first Islamic bank is the Al-Rajahi Bank in Saudi Arabia, which has assets of over $ 25 billion, and granted Islamic credit operation of a value of $21.4 billion. The second Islamic bank in the Arab economy is the Kuwait Finance House (KFH), which was established in 1977, and has 42 branches received a high classification of A from Fitch rating, and A- from Standard and Poor's (KFH, 2006). The variety and the importance of Islamic banks among the top 100 Islamic banks working in the Arab economy also exist as shown in the Table No. 43. The owners' equity of first Islamic bank is about 36 times of the bank ranked number eight, and ranged between $ 3.6 billion and $ 0.1 billion. This observation is also applied to other financial indicators including total assets, granted credits and the total deposits.

Many issues are still facing the Islamic bank in order to enhance its role in the Arab economy. Example of such issues: many major challenges which have not yet been overcome facing Islamic banks. These challenges are related to: finding answers to accounting and managerial issues, to decide how to treat the depositors of the Islamic bank who are not stockholders, bondholders, or creditors; to develop a relevant system to measure annually the profitability of several long-term investment projects in an accurate and a fair way, in order to distribute profits between different classes of depositors; to develop generally accepted policy to determine the dividends policy among stockholders and depositors as long as depositors suppose to participate in accomplished profit; to decide to what extent Islamic banks must follow the central Bank regulations, corporate Laws and generally accepted accounting principles. Finally, to decide how to deal with Basel II regulations regarding capital and risk measures, and how to appraise risk merits of Islamic instruments, securities, bank operations and portfolios. However, recently an attempt was done to articulate generally accounting financial institutions.

Table 43. The top Islamic banks among the top 100 Arab banks in 2005 in $ billion

Top Islamic Banks	Rank	Assets	Credits	Equity	Deposits
Al-Rajahi Bank; SA	5	25.3	21.4	3.6	19.0
Kuwait Finance House	17	16.0	7.2	1.9	10.9
Dubai Islamic Bank; UAE	26	11.7	6.5	1.0	9.1
Al- Baraka Banking group	42	6.3	3.2	0.6	5.2
Abu Dhabi Islamic bank; UAE	44	6.1	1.3	0.7	4.8
Faisal Islamic Bank of Egypt	67	2.9	0.3	0.2	2.2
Qatar Islamic bank	72	2.6	2.1	0.6	1.9
Jordan Islamic bank	80	2.2	1.2	0.1	2.0
Qatar International Islamic bank	88	1.7	0.9	0.24	1.4

Source: UAB (2006) United of Arab Bank Journal; Issue 309; August, 2006; 275-280.

The existence of Islamic banks in the Arab economy and ability to compete with commercial conventional banks received lots of debates and contracted findings. For example, Hassan (2005) found that Islamic banking industry is relatively less efficient compared to conventional banks with an average cost efficiency of 74%, a profit efficiency of 84%, and an average technical efficiency of 84%. While other reports indicated that some Islamic banks have the advantage of high returns for deposits compared to the conventional banks. For example, the distributed rates for different types of deposits ranged from 5.6% to 8.45% in 2006 by KFH as an Islamic bank compared to 4% to 5.5% in the conventional banks for deposits on USD (KFH, 2006).

Second: Takaful (Islamic insurance) firms: at the beginning of the eighties, a new Islamic firm was introduced to the insurance business named as Takaful Corporation. It works based on a cooperative concept between the subscribers and the stockholders of the insurance firm. Today in 2007, there are about 23 Takaful firms working in the Arab economy. Of the total Saudi Arabia has 12 firms; Bahrain 4; Sudan 3, Qatar 2, Tunisia 1, Jordn1, Syria and Palestine I for each under establishment (IIBI, 2007). The Islamic insurance firm works as either in a cooperative legal entity or in form of private and public corporation. The Takaful insurance as conventional insurance includes three groups of insurance. First, the life insurance group which known in Islamic insurance as a family insurance which includes individual programs which may be attached to health insurance, family programs which may be attached with health and/or provident fund or retirement programs. The second group is related to general insurance such as care and vehicles, marine and aviation, liability insurance, work accidents. The third group is reinsurance group known as ReTakaful insurance as existed in the convention insurance business.

The concept of the general insurance based on Takaful is a short term assurance for a specific risk, that the participant will get a compensation for an occurred damaged or loss based on cooperative between all participants on return to pay annual premium considered as donation to the fund of the insurance company. At the end of the fiscal year, the participants are supposed to share the stockholders with any surplus produced from the collected insurance premiums. The Takaful insurance has a special Islamic board such as the case of Islamic bank to monitor the business activities of the firm and to confirm whether business transactions are accorded with Islamic Shariah complaint, and to monitor the distribution of profit between policyholders and stockholders of the Islamic insurance company.

A special statement should be prepared known as the statement of participants' revenues or statement of policyholders, in order to calculate the surplus to be transferred to participants' funds which is called as policyholders' fund. The Takaful Company prepares as a part of its annual report a statement of changes in participants (policyholders) funds, which is similar to the same statement that is prepared to indicate changes in the owners' equity statement of the firm. However, the participants' fund of the general insurance activity should be separated from the fund of policyholders of the family (life) insurance. The Takaful net profit calculating after deducting the reinsurance share and the value of settled claims from the gross contributions paid by participants. The Islamic insurance business has to reinsure in other specialized reinsurance companies, which are qualified for this kind of business and risk. Thus, the re-insurance premiums should be deducted from gross contributions premiums to produce the retained contributions from the policyholders. As conventional insurance firm, the auto insurance represents the highest share of Takaful activities compared to the total premiums of all types of insurances. For example, the share of auto insurance was about 57% of the total premiums of all types of insurance in the Takaful insurance company of Kuwait, followed by 19% for the family insurance, 10% for general accidents, 9% for fire accidents, and 5% for marine and aviation insurance according to its annual report in 2005.

The Takaful business still has a limited share of the Arab insurance market for all types of life and general insurances. It also existed mainly in few Arab states and concentrated in Sudan, Saudi Arabia and other Arab Gulfs, with limited share of the total insurance market, especially with relation to family insurance and reinsurance business. In addition; the majority of the Tukaful insurance firms work in small size of capital which ranged between one million to 60 million, with few exceptions. The gross contributions are paid by the participants as policy holders also have less annual values compared to the conventional incurrence firms, as indicated in Table No. 44, which shows a summary of information about selected Tukaful firms working in different Arab states.

Table 44. Summary for selected Arab Takaful firms in (2004- 2006) in $ Million

	Established Year	Capital	Gross contributions	Assets
Watania Cooperative Insurance; Sudan	1989	1.0		
Takaful Insurance co. Jordan	1996	4.5		
Wethaq Takaful Com. Kuwait	2000	24.0		24.8
Gulf For Takaful Insurance; Kuwait	2004	58.0	5.2	61.0
Takaful International; Bahrain	1989	16.0	13.0	32.0
First Takaful Insurance Com. Kuwait	2000	25.0	29.0	30.0

Sources: The annual reports of the respected companies for years (2004 to 2006).

As indicated in the above table, the Takaful companies in the Arab economy have limited size of assets with limited share of market compared to the conventional insurance companies. The majority of the Takaful companies just was established after 2000, which means they are still in the early stage of such business. However, a multinational Takaful located in Dubai (Islamic Arab insurance company) has decided to increase its capital from $14 million to about $ 300 million in 2006, this company has subsidiaries in Arab states as well as in outside the Arab economy according to its annual report of year 2006. Finally, it may be stated that Islamic insurance business is facing three issues; First; The Takaful business share represents only 6% of the total insurance in the Arab economy, it formed in Sudan about 80% in the total insurance market, but it had 8 % in Saudi Arabia, 2% in UAE, 5% in Jordan, 4% for Qatar and Bahrain. Second; there are no specialized reinsurance Islamic corporations which have lead the Takaful firm to reinsure in conventional insurance firms. Third; very limited size of Islamic life (family) insurance due to Moslems' believes concerning this issue (Bhatty, 2001).

Third: Islamic investment funds: The first introduced Islamic fund in the Arab economy was around 1995, and since that time the number and the total assets values are increasing so rapidly. It is like any mutual fund, which divided into equal shares with minimum value of investment as expressed by the number of shares or by the value of investment. The holders of fund shares known as the investors actually are the owners of the fund. The capital shares of the fund may be traded in the stock exchanges, accordingly, like any corporation the owner holders are changing continuously as a result of trading their own shares. However, the fund runs and is promoted by an Islamic or commercial bank or any financing business corporation. The Islamic fund differs from a traditional fund by the fact that the investments are only in Islamic securities such as equities and Sukuks, and is excluded any fixed income security from its portfolio. Moreover, they are not allowed to be invested in securities issued by firms producing prohibited goods or services according to Islamic Shariah. The Islamic funds are either closed mutual funds are traded in the stock exchanges, or open mutual fund, the Islamic open funds are traded outside the financial market, but few of open funds are also traded in the stock exchange as in the case of Dubai Financial market. Islamic funds considered as growth investment fund, while others are classified as income funds, using either local currency or foreign currencies such as USD, Euro, and Yen. Some Islamic funds include equities from corporations working in the Arab states, while others may include portfolio of both Arab and foreign securities.

Generally speaking, we can say that the Islamic funds including various types based on major functions of the fund, such as; Islamic equity funds, Ijara (leasing) fund, bond funds, balanced funds, and real estate funds, as presented in Table No. 45.

There are about 84 Islamic equity funds traded in the Arab economy and are mainly in the Arab Gulf states markets, 4 Ijarah funs, 2 bond funds, 6 balanced funds, and 7 real estate funds. The majority of Islamic equity funds are initiated in Saudi Arabia, followed by Bahrain and UAE. The Ijarah (leasing) funds are traded only in Saudi Arabia, while the bond funds are traded in Qatar and UAE. The Islamic funds are managed and promoted by Arab Islamic banks, local and foreign commercial banks, and local and foreign investment companies located in

Arab Gulf states. The total assets of existed Islamic funds ranged between $ 5 million to $500 million, and the minimum investment by an investor ranged between $ 2000 and $ 100,000. The manager bank of the fund gets annual fees from 1% to 2% of the total assets (FII; 2007 and 2002). The significance of Islamic investment fund in enhancing Arab economy is a contradictory issue, and economists argue that the Islamic investment funds have the following limitations:

- Islamic investments funds are considered as a circulation of cash flow, with no real value added to the economy,
- May not added to the financial markets as long as the local investors can deal directly with the stock exchanges.
- The minimum investment value for the number of shares and/or the investment value may not attract small and wide range of investors
- The Islamic funds may have less diversification products compared to other finance instruments, due to the fact that their portfolios concentrate in specific products and one or two geographical areas.
- Other critics are related to the content of the portfolio of such investment funds, and if they are all accord with Islamic Shariah, which needs to check all individual corporation activities included in the portfolio.
- In addition, various funds were liquidated just after few years of establishment. Finally, the specialized Islamic funds such that related to leasing and real estate funds are still limited compared to the equity funds.
- Moreover, the value of Islamic fund assets is still limited compared to the conventional mutual investment funds traded in the Arab economies.
- The fees that are collected for trading is high compared to similar activities.

However, in some Arab states foreign investors may buy equities from stock exchanges only through investment funds such as the case of Saudi's stock exchange in which otherwise may not deal directly with.

Table 45. The existed Islamic funds in the Arab economy in 2007 and their holding firms

Types of Islamic	Number	Existed in	Management- Promoter
Murabaha funds	84	Saudi Arabia, UAE, Kuwait, Bahrain; and Qatar	Investment firms Commercial bank Foreign commercial banks Islamic banks
Ijara (leasing) funds	4	Saudi Arabia	Commercial banks Islamic banks Foreign investment firms
Bond (Sukuk) funds	2	UAE and Qatar	Foreign commercial banks
Balanced and hybrid funds	6	Saudi Arabia and UAE	Islamic banks Commercial banks
Real estate funds	7	UAE, Kuwait, Saudi Arabia and Qatar	Investment firms Commercial banks Islamic banks

Source: compiled by the author based on: Institute of Islamic Banking and Insurance http://www.islamic-banking.com and FII: Filaka International (2007); available on line: www.filaka.com

Fourth: Islamic Securities: In the last decade, various new Islamic instruments were introduced to the Arab economy as a way of new channels of financing capital and expansion existing corporations and projects, based on the Islamic Shariah legislation. These securities as all marketable securities may be traded in the Arab stock markets according to the related laws and regulations. They are known as Sukuk or Islamic bonds, which have different maturity terms, and may be connected to a specific project or to a group of projects. In the last case, it called as the joint Sukuk. The Sukuks is security with maturity period attached with annual or semi annual returns supposed to be called as dividends or profit rate. The difference between Islamic Sukuk security from conventional bond is that the bond fixed rate is stated based on the commercial interest rate among other terms of maturity and other characteristics, while the Sukuk rate is calculated based on the expected return of that project which is supposed to be financed by the entire issue of Sukuks securities. However, using the Sukuks or the Islamic instruments or certificates is still at the early stage and located only in the Arab Gulf states with limited values and with few issues. This applies to issuers from governments, financial institutions and public corporations related to the private sector. However, some Islamic economists expect that such securities may be expanded significantly in the near future.

The Sukuks may be issued by various groups, including; First: Arab governments such as in case of Bahrain and Qatar states which issued lately several securities between 2000 and 2005 year, attached to financing specific projects and known as Sovereign Sukuks for short term and long term maturity. Second; it may issue by public corporations which aimed to finance a specific project as a part of the development plan of the corporation. However, these types of Sukuks issues are very limited in the Arab economy, few corporations were used this type of financing. The third group that may issue Sukuk instruments are the financial institutions such as commercial, development and Islamic banks. For example the Islamic Development Bank which is a development fund issued a debt fixed rate Sukuks of US$ 400 million with five years maturity, in order to finance Leasing, installment sale program and Istisna'a activities as indicated in the annual report of 2006 (IDB, 2006).

Chapter 8

OTHER FINANCIAL INSTITUTIONS

Besides the above presented financial institutions, there are still other financial firms have been operating in the Arab economy, even they are less important than the above mentioned institutions, as expressed by the total assets and allocated capital. This group includes six financial institutions which exist in the majority of Arab states, such as the leasing companies, housing and mortgage financing companies, money changers, pension, provident funds and social security corporations, microfinance institutions, and brokerage firms dealing with financial markets.

Financing Leasing firms: Leasing is an instrument of financing private businesses through a contract which permits the lessee to use an equipment, machine, motor, real property or any other assets over a stated or open time period, on return of regular equal or unequal installments, to be paid to the leasing specialized company according to agreed upon terms. The leasing company as the supplier of the asset is playing the role of financing and offering a low cost alternative. The leasing business has many forms and variety of terms and conditions such as leasing ending with ownership, leasing with the right to replace advanced one, operational leasing, leasing thought participation of banks, and other institutes direct finance leasing and leverage leasing.

Financing leasing operation is a well known business in the developed countries with a value of $ 313 billion in 1994, it is used in the developed countries for a long time, but, it is still limited in low and middle income countries with a value of $ 44 billion in 1994. This is also the case in the Arab economy, in spite of the fact that the specialized leasing corporations are existing in some Arab countries such as Jordan, Morocco, Tunisia, and Oman, the leasing value is still immaterial and reached only in Morocco $ 200 million in 1994 as an example

(IFC, 1996). The leasing industry is supposed to play a critical role in financing the economic development in small economies, in which the majority of business firms are either in small or medium scale and may have no access to the formal financial sector such as the commercial banks. The financing leasing instrument may benefit all parties concerned including the leasing company, the lessee, who uses the property and the financing intermediate in case of having a third party.

The use of leasing has some advantages as well as shortages for the leased company. For example, the advantages include saving the needed cash in case of purchasing rather than leasing, the lessee may upgrade the equipment at a minimum cost, there is also the tax advantage for considering annual leasing cost as part of the production cost, and the leasing process may be financed in less cost than direct borrowing from the bank to finance purchasing of new assets. In addition, leasing as a form of financing is most suitable to small scale business firms which represent the majority of Arab economy. For the limitations of using leasing; the lessee has to continue paying lease installments, even if it decided not to continue, and the feeling that the firm does not own the asset.

The insignificant role of leasing as a financing instrument in Arab economy was discussed by various studies. For example, Nasr, (2004) found that the leasing industry is underdeveloped in MENA, despite its potential and asked for a well developed and properly regulated financial leasing sector. The IFC study (IFC, 2005, p. 11) referred the underdevelopment of leasing industry in the developing economies to the absence of clearly defined and predictable laws governing leasing transactions, unclear accounting standards, lack of an appropriate tax regime, impaired funding abilities, and the absence of an appropriate regulatory and supervisory framework. Gallardo (1999) explores the potential of leasing as an option to expand small businesses' access to medium-term financing for capital equipment and new technology.

Mortgage and housing financing markets: The housing sector is considered an important element in the formation of the gross domestic product, in offering job opportunities, serving related industries, supplying the major share of the domestic fixed capital formation. In most countries the housing sector witnesses prosperity as well as depression periods according to the political and economic trends of that particular country. Housing is a major concern of every state, society, and families. For the state it has a political and economic effect, and plays a significant role in developing the economy and creating new jobs. For families, it offers a shelter as well as it fulfills a social function within the society. It is related to finding a shelter to live in, known as a dwelling unit. The demand for private housing units comes from several parties, such as newly formed families, families and individuals need to improve their present dwelling units, and those waiting to replace their dilapidated units. The majority of housing supply comes from private sector the private sector includes households who arrange building their own family housing units as well as the speculative builders and developers who build multi family and commercial housing units for the purposes of reselling or renting (Sabri, 1998b). To finance building housing needs either by households who arrange the construction of their own family or the speculative builders if need long term loans with moderate or low cost, which is not available through formal banking services; thus there is an urgent need to have specialized financial institutions dealing exclusively with financing housing activities.

The specialized housing and the mortgage institutions should be enhanced by both Arab governments and the private sector, which are both considered an essential element in enhancing the housing sector, and to solve the issue of collateral facing the financing processes of acquisition a housing unit, by moderating the related laws and facilitating the existed financing systems to help individuals for getting the needed housing units. In spite of the fact that the residential mortgage market in Arab states is so immaterial and range between 1% of the GDP in Saudi Arabia, 2% in Algeria, 4% for Tunisia, 7% for Morocco, and 11% for Jordan, compared to 50% for the EU states and 65% for USA. However, and just recently, many Arab States opened the public housing finance systems to market competition, leaving private sector in mortgage housing business to grow and to participate in the housing primary market, providing commercial banks with long term loans and extending the interest rate subsidies for mortgages provided through the state-owned housing bank as well as other banks such as that occurred in Jordan, Algeria, Morocco, between 1996 and 2000 as reported by the World Bank study (Word Bank, 2007c).

The Arab mortgage housing system and institutions facing various issues such as; it is mostly public sector in form of government specialized banks, with little contributions from the private sector, and it is not sufficient to meet national needs for residents who are looking for affordable shelters, with inappropriate legal framework. The above observations were supported by various studies. For example, a study examined the mortgage and housing finance market in various MENA countries has reported the need for technical standards to be adopted by Arab governments regarding generally accepted methods of valuations, so that properties are accurately valued on the basis of the price in the open market and to operate on a commercial base (Bahaa Eldin et al. 2004). Another survey found that the Arab home mortgage market is not well developed; the mortgage lending that occurs primarily serves higher-income households, which leads to the need to the development of affordable mortgage loans that serve broad sections of the population (Erbas and Nothaft, 2002).

Money changers Firms: The incompetence of formal financing system leads to increase the role of the informal financing system. The money changers are one of the informal financial systems that operate in the Arab economy, and it is used to be the only source of funding for many borrowers in some Arab states. The money changers perform different tasks such as buying and selling of currencies, money transfers, cashing checks, trading in local stocks, and granting small loans. The money changers play a critical role during the absence of an active banking system. In spite of the fact that the related laws prevent the money changers from accepting deposits or granting loans, we find the money changers conduct such functions for many customers in the Arab economy, since they are considered as small banks with less formality and bureaucracy compared to the official banks. The money changers in Arab economy act in the form of sole firms, partnership, private and public corporations. However, in some cases the money changers are classified into various groups, in which each group assigned for different tasks. The money changers organized the profession based on legal entity and value of prescribed capital and the permitted trading activities, which include exchange currencies, cashing travel and personal checks and sending transfers abroad. The majority of the Arab states control the money changers' operation by the central bank, with less control procedures compared to those measures imposed on the banks. There is no Arab association to unify the Arab money changers such as existed in the insurance and banking sectors, but they may organize at the national level such as the Syndicate for money changers of Lebanon in Beirut. The capital and assets of Arab money changers vary from one firm to another and from Arab state to another, in many Arab states some moneychanger emerged to become banks, stock brokerage companies and to work as multi-purposes financial institutions.

Retail brokers and brokerage firms: To trade with stocks, buyers and sellers may not deal directly with stock exchanges; they have to do that through registered brokers. The broker may be certified individual or authorized company. Today, the majority of the Arab stock exchanges required that dealing with stock exchanges should be through a public or private corporation and no longer an individual broker may deal with stock exchange as used to be, while some stock exchanges such as in Saudi Stock market permit both the banks as well as the brokerage firms to trade in stock market. The brokers are authorized to receive, process, and participate in stating prices, and execute orders in the stock exchanges. The brokerage companies are supposed to work for their own accounts, or for the account of other investors, who open accounts in the brokerage firm and pay minimum amounts. In general; stock brokerage firms are considered significant members in the stock exchanges, and they may participate in the ownership of the stock exchanges partially or fully in many stock exchanges including some of the Arab stock exchanges. In the Arab economy, there are about four hundred brokerage firms dealing with Arab stock markets.

The majority of the Arab stock markets have from 8 to 40 brokerage firms dealing with their respective stock exchange, while in Egypt there are about 130 brokerage firms, in Jordan and UAE there are more than seventy firms for each. The capital of brokerage firm in Arab economy ranged between less than $ one million to over $ 100 million. Examples of the major brokerage companies existed in the Arab economy are: the Kuwait Investment company ($ 170 million), the Kuwait International Investment company ($ 110 million) the Dlala brokerage and investment holding company in Qatar ($ 55 million), and the Amman for Securities Company ($ 90 million). The brokerage firms with capital over than $ 5 million which represent the average capital for brokerage firm in Arab economy usually deal with stock markets for accounts of customers and with limited activity for their own portfolios. The brokerage firms are working under supervision of the financial commission or capital authority as well as under the control corporate controller. The role of brokerage firm in the Arab economy is supposed to serve saving function in the national economy besides handling trading transactions to increase liquidity available to the financial markets and may invest in primary markets, which enhance the economic development of the national economy. The brokerage firms in most of the Arab states are organized in professional association of brokerage firms at the national level, but not at the Arab level as existed in banks, insurance and stock markets. Finally, it should be noted that the stock and bond brokerage business in the Arab economy is still very modest business comparing to international brokerage firms such as Merrill Lynch, BlacRock, Morgan Stanley, and AG Zurich which have over $ one billion in assets for each.

Pension funds and social security corporations: Recently, the role of pension fund is increasing in the world economy as well as in the Arab economy for various reasons; the new concept of social responsibility towards workers including government and private sector employees has been enhanced, thus the need for what is called the social nets or protection plans have been increased to cover their necessities after retirement. The trend towards privatization of retirement government plans and government social security programs is also a new concept, which calls for privatization of retirement programs or at least to be operated in independent legal entities to conduct such funds and programs. The role of the pension funds in saving at the national level which will lead to accumulated fund for investment is also increasing. Accordingly, governments,

NGOs and business sectors using different compensation plans for the benefit of their employees and workers.

Today, in Arab states we find various forms and names for retirement programs, such as government retirement programs, pension funds, provident funds, and social security programs. The concept of such funds and programs regardless of the name is to have some compensation for workers at specific age or at termination of work. The compensation has covered insurance against old age, disability and death; in addition to some systems which also offer non-employment insurance. The sources of funds for the pension funds come from payments of both the employers including government and semi government agencies, professional associations and privet employers as well as from the employees, in addition to the collected returns of the fund investment. The average monthly payment of employee is to pay 5% from their salaries and 10% to be paid from the employers. The compensation may take form of paying monthly installments after retirement age or paying a lump sum as compensation in one deal. The retirement programs existed in the Arab economy may be classified as follows:

- A retirement plan covering military and civil government employees is financed directly by the regular operation budget of the government, without having a special fund. The government includes the retirement payments in single items along with payments to the existing employees. In this case, the employees may or may not pay contribution to the retirement plans.
- A retirement plan covering military and civil government employees is operated by independent special funds. The name of that unit may be pension funds or social security programs. This legal entity receives contributions of both government and employees and invests that in diversification portfolios independently from government budget and interference.
- A retirement plan covering non government employees is operated by independent special funds known as social security corporations or pension funds and is run by either semi government institutions or private sector, in order to protect private employees and labor.
- A retirement plan covering professional employees operated by independent special funds or social security corporations owned by the respective associations such as the association of engineers, physicians, lawyers, chemists, and accountants.

- A retirement plan covering private employees is operated by private pension funds or social security corporations that are owned by private sector and selling their services to private business corporations and self-employments.

Accordingly, we find many public and private pension funds and social security corporations. For example in Jordan, there is the government retirement system for their employees besides the Jordanian social security corporation which is a mandatory self-financed scheme run by the government to cover non-government employees since 1978. In Saudi Arabia; there is the Retirement Pension Fund and the General Organization for Social Insurance, in Algeria there are three pension and social security agencies including CACOBATPH, CASNOS and CNAS, in Tunisia there are two agencies, in Bahrain there are two agencies including the General Organization for Social Insurance and the Pension Fund Commission, in Morocco there are three agencies including the Morocco Pension fund and the PCAR, in Oman there is the Public Authority for social insurance, in UAE there are Abu Dhabi Retirement Pensions and Benefits Fund, the General Pension and Social Security Authority and the National Social Security Authority, in Kuwait there is the Public Institute for Social Security (PIFSS) and so on. The majority of Arab social security corporations and public and private funds join the membership of the international organization known as International Social Security Association (ISSA) located in Geneva.

The above government and private pension funds as well as social security institutions in Arab economy create a significant pool of saving and thus lead that to run and manage billion of USD. For example the total assets of the Jordan Social Security Corporation were more than $ 6 billion in 2006, the local investment for the General Organization for Social Insurance in Saudi Arabia, were $ 6 billion in 2006, and the total assets of the Bahrain Pension Fund Commission were about $ 3.7 billion in 2005 according to their annual reports. In addition, the total enrollment of such funds is increasing significantly, for example the number of enrolled employees in Morocco Pension funds is about 854, 000 participants in 2007. This means that the majority of Arab employees are connected to such funds either as enrolled insured or as retirements.

However, the investment of pension funds and social security corporations mainly located in financial markets including equities and bonds, especially government bonds, and deposits in national and foreign banks. For example, the assets of public pension funds that have invested in government bonds and loans were about 85% of the Egyptian state pension fund, in Lebanon were 50% and Libya were 64% invested in government bonds. This situation is considered a disadvantage, because these funds are diverted away from the real economy toward government deficit financing (World Bank, 2006c). Another issue facing public pension funds is the low return on assets portfolio which may create a burden on the regular government budget to cover shortages. For example, a study (Mohammed, 2002) found that the social insurance schemes in Arab Gulf states facing a continuous escalation in their costs, and suggesting increasing the contribution rates.

Microfinance Institutions: There are many voluntary financial institutions working as NGOs to offer small loans to disadvantage borrowers who are not qualified to deal with the banking system. These institutions are known as microfinance system and considered a part of the informal financing existed in the Arab economy. The Arab microfinance business is also in the early stage, but with high growth potential. Today, in the Arab economy, there are over 75 microfinance institutions providing credit to poor micro entrepreneurs in; Egypt, Jordan, Lebanon, Morocco, Palestine, Tunisia and Syria, Yemen, Algeria, Iraq, Bahrain, Sudan and Saudi Arabia. The majority of the microfinance firms working in Arab states are organized as members or associate members in a regional network called Sanabel, which was established in 2002 by 17 founding members in 7 Arab countries and it is located in Cairo. The Sanabel network works and serves Arab micro finance entrepreneurs, the member of Sanabel network should have a minimum of 5,000 active clients (SANBEL, 2006). The total loan portfolio in microfinance was about $ 243 million distributed in 8 Arab states as shown in Table No. 46. Egypt and Morocco have the highest share of microfinance portfolio, which were over $ 56 million for each, while Yemen had the smallest share of microfinance in the Arab economy in 2003, even there are 15 institutions working in microfinance activities (UNCDF, 2004).

Some microfinance institutions are concentrated on special groups such as women, and rural areas, while others offer their loans to all disadvantage borrowers. The average value of microfinance loans range between $ 300 and $10,000 and in some times, even fall less than $300 (Sabri 2003a). The use of this type of informal financing is under debate by many economists as well as by benchmarking studies and surveys which measuring the performance of microfinance activity. In some countries such as Bangladesh, the microfinance instrument was a successful story, while in Arab states, still in premature process. For example, the UNCDF report (2004) found that most microfinance in Arab states concentrating on business, with the absence of voluntary saving and deposits. However, various measures may be applied to examine the performance of the microfinance instrument in the Arab economy. For example, the number of active borrowers in each institution, share of women borrowers, average loan balances per borrower, gross loan portfolio to total assets. A recent report (MIX, 2006) found that the share of women in microfinance portfolio reached 88% in the Arab economy, while the gross loan portfolio to total assets ratio was about 71%, with profit margin of 10%.

Another issue which may be considered as a disadvantage in this business is the major source of revenues, which comes to the Arab microfinance institutions from foreign organizations with limited support of national organizations, or from the Arab governments. The Arab government budgets should allocate more appropriations to the disadvantage borrowers in order to enhance this part of society.

Table 46. The microfinance portfolio loans in the Arab economy at the end of 2003

Arab states	Number of firms	portfolio loans in $ million
Egypt	20	56
Morocco	7	61
Syria	6	43
Tunisia	2	36
Lebanon	6	11
Palestine	7	12
Jordan	5	22
Yemen	15	1
Total	68	243

Source; UNCDF (2004).

Chapter 9

CONCLUSION

Various major conclusions may be pointed out after investigating the Arab financial sector in general and the Arab financial institutions in particular, which may be summarized as follows:

First: the role of commercial bank is still considered as number one among the financial institutions working in the Arab financial sector, in spite of the variety of the financial institutions which existed in the Arab economy. However, it should be noted that the role of commercial bank had been decreased notably, when many of the investors moved their deposits to mutual and investment funds and to private saving corporations all over the world, due to the decreasing interest rate to the lowest level such as 1% on USD and almost zero in the Yen during the period between 2003 and 2005. The increasing role of the mutual and investment funds was on the account of the commercial banks. Nevertheless, this side effect did not remove the commercial bank to be as the most active and efficient depositary institutions in the world's financial sector. This is due to the fact that many of the investment and mutual funds which attract investors are owned and operated by the commercial banks. However, banks may be successful as depository institutions, but they have moderate role in enhancing the Arab economy, since they directed their loans to public sector, large private corporations, short term loans and concentrating on financing of commercial and services sectors rather than industrial and agricultural sectors.

Second: the importance of the Arab financial institutions is different compared to the world economy, with exception of the commercial banks. The order and importance of the other Arab financial institutions are different from that existed in the world economy as expressed by capital, total assets and revenues, as shown in Table No. 47. It indicates that commercial bank is considered number one in both Arab and world economies, while the ranking of life insurance firms, leasing companies, and development funds are so different. The life insurance firms represent the second important institutions among the world economy; while rank number nine in the Arab economy. This is also applied to the development funds and Islamic banks, which represent the second and the third important financial institutions as expressed by the owners' equity and the total assets in the Arab economy. While such institutions are ranked as eighth and eleventh in the world economy, in which they less important and have minor role in the financial sector in the world context as expressed by their total assets compared to other types of financial institutions.

Third: In spite of the new developments occurred in the financial institutions such as the privatization of public banks, and opening the financial sectors to private and foreign institutions in some Arab states such as Syria, Algeria, Iraq, and Egypt, the size of the financial sector in the Arab economy is still limited compared to the world financial sector. For example, the top ten Arab banks have assets ranged between $39 billion and $25 billion for each, compared to the top ten world banks which have assets value ranged from $ 833 billion to over $ one trillion for each such as Citigroup bank, JPMorgan Chase, Bank of America, HSBC, and Mitsubishi UFJ Financial Group, according to the Banker ranking. The Arab insurance sector is also much less when it compared to the respective sector at the world level, considering their capital and owner equity, the total assets and the annual revenues of insurance premiums for all types of insurances.

Fourth: the role of Islamic institutions and instruments is still limited for about 10% or less of the Arab financial sector. Considering the fact that there are continuous increasing in Islamic finance activities occurred in the last decade, as expressed by Islamic investment funds which deal with both Islamic instruments and equity securities, emerging the Islamic insurance companies (Takaful) and developing of some of the Islamic banks to be from the list of the top 100 Arab banks. But such improvements are still modest compared to the conventional financing activities in the Arab economy. For example, One Islamic Bank in Arab economy included in the first top ten Arab banks, and another one ranked in the next ten banks, as well as another rank among the next third ten ranked banks in Arab economy (UAB, 2006).This is also more valid in case of insurance activities, which may be at pre-mature stage and early to be judged.

Fifth: the weak role of some financial institutions in the Arab economy such as the leasing corporations, the life insurance businesses and the brokerage companies compared to the size and importance of those institutions in the world economy. For example, the role and size of life insurance, property, casualty and the reinsurance corporations in the Arab economy is so immaterial compared to the insurance business in the world economy. For example, the annual direct premium value in the top Arab life insurance firms ranged between $ 10 million to $ 300 million, compared to the top world insurance companies, which ranged between $ 139 billion to $45 billion for each in 2004, such as ING Group (Netherland), AXA (France), Assicurazioni Generali (Italy), Aviva (UK), Prudentia (UK), Nippon Life Insurance (Japan), Legal and General Group (UK), CNP Assurances (France), MetLife (USA)and Dai-ichi Mutual Life Insurance of Japan (III, 2007).

Table 47. Rank of Arab financial institutions compared to the world economy

	Rank in Arab Economy	Rank in World Economy
Commercial banks	1	1
Insurance companies -Life	9	2
Investment, Trust and Saving firms	8	5
Pension funds	5	4
Development funds and specialized banks	2	8
Mutual and investment funds	6	6
Brokers firms	10	7
Insurance companies -general	4	3
Leasing companies	12	9
Money changers	7	10
Islamic banks	3	11
Islamic insurance firms (Tukaful)	11	12

Source: compiled by the Author

Sixth: The Islamic financial institutions are co-existed among the conventional financial institutions with small share in the Arab economy markets compared to the total share of the conventional financial institutions, with exception of the Sudan, in which the Islamic institutions have significant role in its economy, with a low percentage for conventional finance activities. The Islamic funds and Sukuks and other forms of Islamic securities are existed mainly in the Arab Gulf states and Sudan.

REFERENCES

Abed, George T. and Hamid R. Davoodi (2003) *Challenges of Growth and Globalization in the Middle East and North Africa* (International Monetary Fund, Washington, D. C.).

AFESD (2005) *Arab Fund for Economic and Social Development Annual Report*, 2005 (AFESD, Kuwait).

AMF (2005) *Arab Monterey Fund Annual Report 2005* (Arab Monterey Fund, UAE).

AMF (2006a) *Unified Arab Economic Report: 2006* (League of Arab State, Arab Monetary Fund, Arab Fund for Economic and social Development and AOPEC, September 2006, UAE).

AMF (2006b) *AMDB Quarterly Bulletin No. 48* (Arab Monterey Fund, UAE).

ANRDI (2004) *Arab National and Regional Development Institutions 2004. (A Profile, Kuwait).*

BADEA (2005) *Arab Bank for Economic Development in Africa Annual Report*, 2005 (BADEA. Khartoum, Sudan).

Bahaa Eldin, Ziad, Mahmoud Mohieldin and Sahar Nasr (2004) *Prospects Of Mortgage Markets In MENA Countries: An Analysis of Financial, Legal and Institutional Aspects With Emphasis on the Egyptian Case Study* (Working Paper 0430, World Bank).

BDL (2006) *Banque Du Liban Annual Report; Statistical Annex* (Bank of Lebanon, Beirut, Lebanon).

BDL (2006) *Banque Du Liban Annual Report; Statistical Annex* (Bank of Lebanon, Beirut, Lebanon).

Benbouziane, M. and A Benamar, (2007) *The impact of exchange rate regime on the real sector in MENA countries* (Université Abou Bekr Belkaid, Tlemcen, Algeria).

Bhatty, Mohammad Ajmal (2001) *Takaful Industry: Global Profile and Trends*, 2001 (Takaful International, Bahrain).

BIS (2006a) *International Convergence of Capital Measurement and Capital Standards* (Bank for International Settlements, Switzerland.

CBB (2006) *Central Bank of Bahrain Annual Report*, 2006 (Central Bank of Bahrain, Bahrain).

CBE (2006) *Central Bank of Egypt Annual Report 2005-2006* (Central Bank of Egypt, Cairo, Egypt).

CBI (2006) *Central Bank of Iraq; Annual Bulletin* (Statistics and Research Department, CBI, Baghdad, Iraq).

CBK (2006) *The Thirty fourth annual report of the Central Bank of* Kuwait; 2005-2006 (CBK, Kuwait).

CBS (2006) *Central Bank of Sudan Annual Report 2006* (Bank of Sudan, Khartoum, Sudan).

Creane, Susan, Rishi Goyal, A. Mushfiq Mobarak and Randa Sab (2004) *"Financial Development in the Middle East and North Africa"* (IMF Working Paper, International Monetary Fund, Washington, D. C.).

Elkelish, Walaa Wahid and Andrew P. Marshall (2006) "Financial Structure Choice in the United Arab Emirates Emerging Market" *International Journal of Business Research*, 6 (1); 15-30.

Eltony, M. (2003) *Arab financial sector development and institutions; the implications of financial sector reform in Arab countries on economic development* (Economic Research Forum, Egypt).

Erbas, S. Nuri and Frank E. Nothaft (2002*) The Role of Affordable Mortgages in Improving Living Standards and Stimulating Growth: A Survey of Selected MENA Countries* (IMF Working Paper WP/02/17, International Monetary Fund, Washington, D. C.).

FEDWIRE (2006) Funds Transfer System: Assessment of Compliance with the Core Principles for Systemically Important Payment Systems, *(Working paper*, USA).

FII (2002) *Islamic Equity Funds: analysis and Observations on the Current State of the Industry* (Failaka International Inc., available in www. Filaka).

FII (2007) Failaka International Inc. London; available on line:www.filaka.com.

GAIF (2007) General Arab Insurance Federation, available on line http://www.gaif-1.org

Gallardo, Joselito, (1999) "*Leasing to Support Small Businesses and Micro enterprises*" (November 30, World Bank Policy Research Working Paper No. 1857).

Ghosh, Atish R., Jonathan D. Ostry, Anne-Marie Gulde, and Holger C. Wolf (1997) *Does the Exchange Rate Regime Matter for Inflation and Growth?* (International Monetary Fund, Washington, D. C.).

Hakim, S. and S. Neaime, (2005) *A Unified risk assessment of commercial banks in the MENA region Risk management policies across MENA countries* (Economic Research Forum, Egypt).

IDB (2006) *Islamic Development Bank Annual Report of 2006* (Islamic Development Bank, Jeddah).

IFC (1996) *Leasing in Emerging Markets* (International Finance Corporation, World Bank, Washington D. C.).

IFC (2005) *Leasing in Development; Lessons from Emerging Economies by Matthew Fletcher, Rachel Freeman, Murat Sultanov, and Umedjan Umarov* (International Finance Corporation, Washington, D. C).

III (2007) *The III Insurance Factbook 2007* (Insurance Information Institute, New York, USA).

IMF (2006a) *World Economic and Financial Surveys Global Financial Stability Report, Market Developments and Issues* (September, International Monetary Fund, Washington D. C).

IMF (2006c) *World Economic Outlook Database*, (September, International Monetary Fund, Washington D. C.).

IMF (2007a) *World Economic and Financial Surveys Global Financial Stability Report, Market Developments and Issues* (April, International Monetary Fund, Washington D. C).

IMF (2007b) *De facto Classification of Exchange Rate Regimes and Monetary Policy Framework* (International Monetary Fund, Washington D. C).

Jasimuddi, Sajjad M. (2001), "Saudi Arab Banks on the Web" *Journal of Internet Banking and Commerce,* 6, (1).

Jbili, Abdelali and Vitali Kramarenko (2003) *Choosing Exchange Regimes in the Middle East and North Africa* (International Monetary Fund, Washington, D. C.).

Khalfan, Abdulwahed Mo. Sh. Yaqoub S.Y. AlRefaei, and Majed Al-Hajery (2006) "Factors influencing the adoption of internet banking in Oman: a descriptive case study analysis" *International Journal of Financial Services Management,* 1 (2-3); 155-172.

Limam, I. (2001) *A comparative study of GCC banks technical efficiency* (Economic Research Forum, Egypt).

MIX (2006) *Benchmarking Arab Microfinance 2004* (Microfinance Information exchange Inc. Washington, D. C.).

Mohammed, Zakariya Sultan, (2002) "Social Insurance Schemes in the Gulf Countries" *International Social Security Review* 55; 157-169.

Nasr, Sahar (2004) *Financial Leasing In MENA Region: An Analysis Of Financial, Legal And Institutional Aspects* (Working Paper 0424, Economic Research Forum, Egypt).

OAPEC (2006). *Annual Statistics Report, 2006* (Organization of Arab Petroleum Exporting Countries, Kuwait).

OPEC (2002) "*Fund for International Development; OPEC Aid Institutions A Profile 2002*" (OPEC, Vienna).

QCB (2006) *Quarterly Statistical Bulletin*, (Qatar Central Bank, January, Doha, Qatar).

Rehman, Sajjad ur (2006) "IT applications in Kuwaiti financial companies: an analysis" *Information Management and Computer Security* 14; 267-484.

Sabri, Nidal Rashid (1997) *Regional Financial Institutions, the Role of Arab Development Funds* (PCRS, Palestine) 1997.

Sabri, Nidal Rashid (1998a) "Financial Analysis of the Palestinian Industry" *Small Business Economics* 11; 293-301.

Sabri, Nidal Rashid (2003a). "Financing of Palestinian Private Sector" *Arab Journal of Administration* 23; 129- 156.

Sabri, Nidal Rashid and Rania Jaber (2006) "Financial Polices Issues"" in Sabri, Nidal Rashid (2006) Editor *Palestine Country Profile* (Economic Research Forum, and Institut de La Méditerranée, France, 2006).

SAMA, (2006) *Saudi Arab Monetary Agency Annual Report*, 30th of June 2006. (Saudi Arab Monetary Agency, Riyadh).

SANABEL (2006) *Sanabel Annual Report of* 2005; (Microfinance Network for Arab countries, Sanabel, Giza, Egypt).

SWIFT (2006) *SWIFT Annual Report,2006* (Society for Worldwide Interbank Financial Telecommunication, Belgium).

Tawadros, George B. (2007) "Testing the hypothesis of long-run money neutrality in the Middle East" *Journal of Economic Studies* 34 (1); 13 – 28.

UAB (2006) *United of Arab Banks Journal (*Issue No. 309; August) 275-280

UNCDF (2004) *Judith Brandsma and Deena Burjorjee Microfinance in the Arab States Building inclusive financial sectors* (United Nations Capital Development Fund).

World Bank (2006a) *Global Development Finance; The Development Potential of Surging Capital Flows* (The World Bank and Oxford University Press).

World Bank (2006b) *World Development Report 2006; Equity and Development* (The World Bank and Oxford University Press).

World Bank (2006c) *Middle East and North Africa* Region; Economic Developments and Prospects; Financial Markets in A New Age of Oil (World Bank, Washington D. C.).

World Bank (2007c) Middle East and North Africa; Economic Developments and Prospects 2006 Financial Markets in a New Age of Oil *(*Middle East and North Africa Region Office of the Chief Economist, World Bank, Washington C. D.).

Yasin, Mahmoud M. and Ugur Yavas (2007) "An analysis of E-business practices in the Arab culture: Current inhibitors and future strategies" *Cross Cultural Management: An International Journal* 14 (1); 68 – 73.

INDEX

A

Abu Dhabi, 19, 23, 28, 38, 39, 40, 41, 44, 45, 50, 58, 71
access, 18, 29, 34, 66
accidents, 48, 49, 52, 59
accounting, 5, 28, 29, 33, 56, 57, 66
accounting standards, 66
accuracy, 29
AD, 19
adaptation, 19
adjustment, 10
administration, 25, 51
AE, 54, 63
AFM, 41
Africa, 24, 39, 40, 41, 42, 44
age, 49, 70
agent, 19
agricultural, 1, 31, 34, 75
agricultural sector, 1, 31, 75
agriculture, 24, 40, 48
aid, 38
AIM, 47, 48
Algeria, 2, 9, 10, 14, 15, 24, 28, 29, 32, 34, 49, 50, 67, 71, 72, 76
alternative, 65
AMF, 3, 6, 7, 9, 19, 21, 22, 34, 38, 40, 41, 44, 45
appropriations, 40, 73
Arab countries, 9, 28, 47, 49, 53, 65, 72

Arabia, 2, 9, 10, 11, 14, 15, 16, 22, 27, 28, 30, 31, 32, 33, 47, 49, 50, 51, 53, 54, 57, 58, 60, 61, 63, 67, 71, 72
Arabs, 41
arbitrage, 55
arbitration, 5
Asia, 40
Asian, 41, 54
assets, 15, 16, 17, 18, 19, 21, 22, 24, 27, 34, 42, 43, 50, 56, 57, 60, 61, 62, 65, 66, 68, 69, 71, 73, 75, 76
associations, 7, 24, 70
ATM, 27
authority, 15, 25, 69
availability, 30
aviation, 59
awareness, 30

B

Baghdad, 38
Bahrain, 2, 4, 9, 10, 14, 15, 16, 23, 25, 26, 29, 30, 32, 53, 54, 58, 60, 61, 63, 64, 71, 72
balance sheet, 13
Bangladesh, 72
bank financing, 34
Bank of America, 23, 76
banking, 2, 11, 14, 17, 19, 21, 22, 23, 24, 25, 26, 27, 28, 29, 30, 31, 32, 33, 34, 47, 54, 55, 56, 57, 58, 63, 67, 68, 72

banking industry, 29, 58
banks, 2, 3, 4, 5, 6, 7, 11, 12, 13, 14, 15, 16, 17, 18, 19, 21, 22, 23, 24, 25, 26, 27, 28, 29, 30, 31, 32, 33, 34, 39, 42, 43, 47, 53, 54, 55, 56, 57, 58, 61, 63, 64, 65, 66, 67, 68, 69, 71, 75, 76, 77
Basel II, 25, 57
benchmarking, 72
BIS, 19
bondholders, 57
bonds, 3, 11, 13, 14, 15, 16, 42, 43, 53, 54, 55, 63, 71
borrowers, 68, 72, 73
borrowing, 66
British, 4, 28
brokerage, 65, 68, 69, 76
bureaucracy, 68
business, 2, 34, 40, 47, 48, 49, 50, 51, 52, 55, 58, 59, 60, 61, 65, 66, 67, 69, 70, 71, 72, 73, 77
business environment, 49, 52

C

capital, 7, 15, 16, 17, 18, 19, 21, 24, 25, 38, 39, 40, 42, 45, 49, 51, 55, 56, 57, 60, 61, 63, 65, 66, 68, 69, 75, 76
capital flows, 24
car accidents, 48
cash flow, 62
causality, 50
CBI, 12
CBS, 11, 12
central bank, 5, 7, 11, 12, 13, 14, 15, 16, 17, 19, 25, 26, 31, 34, 42, 56, 68
Central Bank, v, 6, 7, 13, 15, 16, 26
channels, 19, 63
children, 39
circulation, 11, 62
civil law, 4
classes, 57
classification, 24, 57
classified, 3, 24, 27, 29, 37, 43, 47, 61, 68, 70
clients, 52, 56, 72
Co, 4, 6, 8, 9

codes, 4
collateral, 27, 32, 37, 67
commerce, 30
commercial, 4, 5, 7, 16, 20, 22, 25, 26, 28, 34, 37, 39, 42, 43, 55, 58, 61, 63, 64, 66, 67, 75
commercial bank, 5, 7, 20, 22, 25, 26, 37, 42, 43, 61, 63, 66, 67, 75
commodity, 56
common law, 4
compensation, 7, 49, 52, 59, 70
competition, 29, 67
composite, 9, 10
composition, 5
computers, 29
concentration, 17
concessional terms, 39, 40, 42, 43
confidentiality, 30
Congress, iv
consolidation, 29
constant rate, 9
construction, 17, 56, 67
contingency, 44
continuity, 42
contracts, 12
control, 4, 6, 14, 17, 31, 56, 68, 69
coordination, 7, 19, 39
corporate governance, 5
corporations, 5, 7, 17, 24, 26, 27, 40, 43, 47, 49, 50, 51, 53, 54, 61, 63, 64, 65, 68, 69, 70, 71, 75, 76
costs, 72
courts, 52
covering, 25, 57, 70, 71
credit, 2, 12, 14, 16, 17, 18, 21, 22, 24, 25, 26, 28, 29, 31, 32, 34, 55, 57, 72
credit card, 12, 29, 35
creditors, 21, 57
cultural, 49
culture, 32
currency, 1, 2, 4, 5, 8, 9, 10, 11, 13, 14, 16, 18, 19, 25, 61
currency board, 14
currency boards, 14
current account, 11, 16, 27, 56

customers, 6, 11, 21, 25, 27, 29, 30, 34, 49, 55, 56, 68, 69

D

DA, 37, 43
death, 49, 70
debt, 12, 14, 24, 25, 29, 34, 42, 54, 64
decisions, 16, 34
deficit, 72
definition, 40
degree, 1, 2, 3, 24, 28, 33
demand, 11, 25, 66
deposit accounts, 11, 43
deposits, 2, 5, 6, 11, 16, 18, 19, 21, 22, 27, 31, 33, 34, 42, 54, 55, 57, 58, 68, 71, 72, 75
depreciation, 11
depression, 66
devaluation, 9
developed countries, 49, 65
developing countries, 24, 31, 39, 40
Development Assistance, 37, 43
development banks, 39
direct investment, 10, 52
disability, 70
discipline, 25
disclosure, 5, 25
discounting, 21
discounts, 35
distribution, 56, 59
diversification, 62, 70
dividends, 57, 63
draft, 55
duties, 17

E

earnings, 34
e-banking, 30
e-commerce, 30
economic, 1, 2, 3, 4, 7, 9, 10, 14, 19, 31, 34, 38, 39, 40, 41, 42, 45, 51, 54, 66, 69
economic development, 42, 66, 69
economic growth, 2, 3

economic performance, 9, 10
economies, 10, 23, 25, 30, 34, 42, 51, 62, 66, 76
economy, 1, 2, 3, 5, 7, 8, 9, 10, 11, 12, 14, 15, 17, 19, 21, 22, 23, 24, 26, 27, 29, 30, 31, 32, 33, 34, 37, 39, 40, 41, 42, 47, 48, 49, 50, 51, 53, 54, 57, 58, 60, 61, 62, 63, 64, 65, 66, 68, 69, 70, 71, 72, 73, 75, 76, 77
education, 49
Egypt, 2, 4, 7, 9, 10, 11, 12, 14, 15, 16, 17, 22, 23, 24, 28, 30, 31, 32, 33, 34, 47, 48, 49, 50, 51, 53, 58, 69, 72, 73, 76
Egyptian, 11, 34, 48, 71
electronic, iv, 12, 14, 29, 30
electronic transfer system, 12
electrostatic, iv
emerging economies, 3
employees, 6, 25, 30, 47, 69, 70, 71
employers, 70
employment, 47, 70
energy, 40
engineering, 48
enrollment, 71
entrepreneurs, 72
environment, 32, 49, 52
equipment, 56, 65, 66
equities, 23, 38, 40, 43, 54, 57, 61, 62, 71
equity, 2, 5, 14, 18, 21, 22, 25, 27, 34, 38, 40, 42, 43, 44, 45, 50, 53, 54, 57, 59, 61, 62, 76
estates, 33
EU, 67
Euro, 25, 61
Europe, 40
European, 31, 54
exchange rate, 9, 10, 14
exchange rates, 10, 14
expenditures, 21, 42
expert, iv
exports, 10

F

family, 49, 59, 60, 61, 67
Federal Reserve, 30
Federal Reserve Bank, 30

fees, 16, 37, 62
finance, 2, 17, 24, 31, 39, 42, 53, 54, 57, 62,
    64, 65, 66, 67, 72, 76, 77
financial crises, 25
financial development, 2
financial institution, 1, 2, 3, 4, 5, 6, 7, 8, 16,
    19, 31, 37, 47, 53, 55, 57, 58, 63, 64, 65,
    67, 68, 72, 75, 76, 77
financial institutions, 1, 2, 3, 4, 5, 6, 7, 8, 16,
    19, 31, 37, 47, 53, 55, 57, 58, 63, 64, 65,
    67, 68, 72, 75, 76, 77
financial loss, 49
financial markets, 1, 4, 5, 8, 62, 65, 69, 71
financial sector, 1, 2, 3, 4, 5, 6, 23, 49, 53, 66,
    75, 76
financial system, 6, 11, 21, 48, 68
financing, 2, 4, 21, 31, 33, 34, 39, 40, 42, 45,
    54, 56, 61, 63, 64, 65, 66, 67, 68, 72, 75, 76
fire, 48, 59
firms, 6, 7, 16, 31, 47, 48, 49, 50, 51, 52, 53,
    54, 58, 60, 61, 63, 65, 66, 68, 69, 72, 73,
    76, 77
fixed interest securities, 55
fixed rate, 63, 64
flexibility, 10
floating, 9, 10
flow, 62
foreign banks, 6, 7, 16, 25, 29, 34, 71
foreign direct investment, 10, 52
foreign exchange, 10, 14, 19, 25
foreign exchange market, 10
foreign investment, 61
France, 47, 51, 77
fraud, 25
fund transfers, 31
funding, 42, 66, 68
funds, 3, 4, 5, 6, 7, 14, 15, 16, 17, 21, 22, 25,
    30, 34, 37, 38, 39, 40, 41, 42, 43, 44, 48,
    53, 54, 55, 56, 59, 61, 62, 63, 65, 69, 70,
    71, 75, 76, 77

G

GCC, 29

generally accepted accounting principles, 5,
    33, 57
Geneva, 71
Germany, 51, 52
GNP, 22
gold, 5, 11, 13, 16, 19
governance, 5
government, 5, 6, 7, 11, 13, 14, 15, 16, 17, 19,
    22, 24, 26, 31, 37, 38, 40, 48, 63, 64, 67,
    69, 70, 71, 73
government budget, 17, 70, 72, 73
governors, 19
grants, 39, 41
gross domestic product (GDP), 2, 3, 10, 21,
    22, 31, 33, 49, 66, 67
group work, 7
groups, 3, 5, 6, 27, 29, 39, 47, 48, 59, 64, 68,
    72
growth, 2, 3, 10, 61, 72

H

handling, 69
health, 48, 49, 51, 59
health insurance, 48, 51, 59
high growth potential, 72
higher-income, 67
holding company, 69
House, 57, 58
households, 67
housing, 25, 65, 66, 67
human, 39
human development, 39
hybrid, 53, 63
hypothesis, 11

I

IBD, 44
implementation, 28
imports, 10, 21
income, 16, 27, 30, 34, 42, 49, 57, 61, 65, 67
independence, 14
indicators, 30, 33, 44, 57

indices, 5
industrial, 1, 34, 75
industry, 24, 29, 40, 58, 66
inflation, 10, 14, 20
information systems, 28
injury, iv
insecurity, 30
instability, 49
institutions, 1, 4, 5, 6, 7, 14, 19, 26, 30, 34,
    65, 67, 70, 71, 72, 73, 75, 76, 77
instruments, 1, 6, 11, 54, 55, 56, 58, 62, 63,
    64, 76
insurance, 4, 5, 6, 7, 16, 27, 47, 48, 49, 50, 51,
    52, 53, 54, 58, 59, 60, 68, 69, 70, 71, 72,
    76, 77
insurance companies, 5, 48, 51, 52, 60, 76, 77
integration, 37
interest rates, 19, 34
interference, 70
international, 13, 14, 19, 25, 30, 49, 51, 56,
    69, 71
international financial institutions, 19
International Monetary Fund (IMF), IMF, 2,
    3, 10, 11, 13, 14, 16, 19, 27, 28, 33, 43
internet, 27, 29, 30
investment, 1, 5, 7, 16, 17, 18, 25, 39, 42, 51,
    53, 54, 55, 56, 57, 61, 62, 63, 69, 70, 71,
    75, 76, 77
investment bank, 25
investors, 3, 5, 7, 54, 61, 62, 68, 75
Iraq, 10, 12, 14, 15, 16, 24, 31, 32, 38, 40, 41,
    47, 72, 76
Islam, 54
Islamic, v, 3, 4, 6, 7, 24, 26, 38, 39, 40, 41,
    42, 43, 44, 45, 48, 53, 54, 55, 56, 57, 58,
    59, 60, 61, 62, 63, 64, 76, 77
Italy, 77

J

Japan, 49, 50, 51, 77
jobs, 66
joint ventures, 56

Jordan, 2, 4, 9, 10, 11, 14, 15, 16, 22, 23, 24,
    27, 28, 30, 32, 33, 34, 47, 50, 53, 54, 58,
    60, 61, 65, 67, 69, 71, 72, 73
Jordanian, 22, 48, 71
jurisdiction, 2, 3, 5, 32
jurisdictions, 5

K

Kuwait, 2, 9, 10, 12, 14, 15, 16, 22, 23, 24,
    25, 27, 28, 30, 31, 32, 33, 37, 38, 41, 50,
    54, 57, 58, 59, 60, 63, 69, 71

L

labor, 70
land, 16, 17
large banks, 29
Latin America, 40
laundry, 31
law, 4, 5, 17, 18, 19
laws, 1, 3, 4, 5, 6, 13, 14, 21, 25, 39, 47, 56,
    63, 66, 67, 68
lawyers, 70
lead, 11, 25, 33, 39, 55, 61, 69, 71
Lebanon, 2, 4, 7, 9, 10, 11, 12, 14, 15, 16, 22,
    27, 28, 30, 31, 32, 33, 34, 47, 49, 50, 51,
    68, 71, 72, 73
legislation, 4, 63
lending, 5, 23, 56, 67
liability insurance, 48, 59
liberalization, 3
Libya, 2, 9, 10, 15, 16, 17, 24, 27, 31, 32, 49,
    50, 71
licenses, 14, 29
limitations, 44, 62, 66
liquidation, 14, 33, 56
liquidity, 5, 11, 14, 17, 21, 25, 69
loans, 14, 16, 17, 18, 19, 21, 22, 24, 25, 27,
    31, 32, 33, 34, 37, 38, 39, 40, 41, 42, 43,
    44, 45, 55, 56, 67, 68, 71, 72, 73, 75
long-term, 56, 57
losses, 11, 33, 48, 49

M

M1, 11
machines, 27
macroeconomic, 9
macroeconomic policy, 9
magnetic, iv, 29
management, 25, 28, 29, 30, 33, 42, 43, 48
manufacturing, 56
maritime, 48
market, 2, 3, 5, 6, 7, 10, 20, 25, 27, 30, 34, 52,
   56, 60, 61, 67, 68
market capitalization, 2, 3
market discipline, 25
market share, 27
markets, 1, 2, 3, 4, 5, 8, 29, 61, 62, 63, 65, 66,
   69, 71, 77
Mauritania, 2, 9, 10, 15, 16, 17, 24, 31, 32
measures, 17, 18, 25, 27, 28, 42, 43, 57, 68,
   72
mechanical, iv
membership, 4, 5, 71
mentoring, 17
mergers, 29
messages, 30
Middle East, 24, 50
middle income, 34, 65
military, 70
Mitsubishi, 76
monetary policy, 13
monetary union, 9
money, 1, 4, 7, 10, 11, 12, 14, 31, 54, 65, 68
money supply, 11
Morocco, 2, 4, 10, 11, 14, 15, 22, 24, 27, 28,
   32, 33, 47, 48, 49, 50, 51, 65, 67, 71, 72, 73
mortgage, 24, 65, 67
mortgages, 67
mutual funds, 61, 75

N

national, 1, 3, 4, 6, 7, 8, 11, 12, 13, 14, 16, 17,
   19, 21, 25, 27, 29, 33, 38, 47, 49, 51, 67,
   68, 69, 71, 73

nationality, 24
net income, 16, 57
Netherlands, 49, 50, 51
network, 31, 72
New York, iii, iv, 31
New York Times, 31
NGOs, 70, 72
Nixon, 13

O

observations, 67
Official Development Assistance, 37, 43
offshore, 25
oil, 7, 22, 37
old age, 70
Oman, 2, 9, 10, 15, 16, 22, 31, 32, 33, 50, 65,
   71
OPEC, 38, 40, 41, 42
openness, 2
organ, 5
organization, 5, 13, 19, 21, 24, 30, 71
organizations, 13, 25, 73
ownership, 17, 18, 24, 29, 39, 65, 69

P

Palestine, 7, 10, 15, 18, 30, 31, 32, 33, 34, 48,
   50, 53, 56, 58, 72, 73
partnership, 7, 47, 68
pegged exchange rate, 9, 10
pension, 4, 7, 16, 65, 69, 70, 71
pensions, 4
per capita, 49
perception, 29
performance, 9, 10, 27, 30, 41, 43, 50, 57, 72
permit, 25, 68
personal, 33, 48, 68
philosophy, 55
physicians, 70
play, 66, 68
PMA, 18
PNA, 18
political, 3, 49, 52, 66

political aspects, 3
poor, 55, 72
population, 67
portfolio, 16, 56, 61, 62, 72, 73
portfolios, 16, 58, 62, 69, 70
power, 11, 26
powers, 26
premium, 37, 48, 49, 50, 51, 52, 59, 77
premiums, 5, 49, 51, 59, 76
preparation, iv
pressure, 31
prices, 5, 22, 37, 68
private, 6, 7, 14, 21, 22, 24, 29, 33, 34, 37, 40,
    47, 58, 64, 65, 66, 67, 68, 69, 70, 71, 75, 76
private banks, 14, 24, 29
private sector, 22, 33, 34, 37, 40, 47, 64, 67,
    69, 70, 71
privatization, 69, 76
privet, 70
procedures, 3, 5, 17, 32, 52, 68
producers, 2
production, 66
productivity, 10
productivity growth, 10
profession, 68
profit, 16, 17, 18, 26, 27, 28, 33, 43, 54, 55,
    56, 57, 58, 59, 63, 73
profit margin, 73
profitability, 27, 57
profits, 15, 16, 27, 56, 57
program, 31, 64
promote, 19
property, iv, 47, 48, 49, 66, 76
prosperity, 39, 42, 66
protection, 5, 21, 49, 69
public, 4, 6, 7, 11, 14, 16, 21, 22, 24, 29, 31,
    34, 40, 47, 58, 63, 64, 67, 68, 71, 75, 76
public corporations, 7, 63, 64, 68
public debt, 14
public housing, 67
public pension, 6, 71
public sector, 31, 34, 67, 75
purchasing power, 11

Q

Qatar, 2, 9, 10, 11, 12, 14, 15, 16, 24, 25, 31,
    32, 34, 49, 50, 51, 53, 54, 58, 61, 63, 64, 69

R

range, 62, 67, 72
real estate, 25, 26, 33, 56, 61, 62
real property, 65
reforms, 28
regional, 6, 7, 19, 25, 38, 43, 72
regular, 65, 70, 72
regulation, 2
regulations, 2, 3, 4, 5, 14, 17, 19, 24, 25, 47,
    54, 57, 63
regulatory bodies, 7
regulatory capital, 27
reinsurance, 7, 47, 48, 49, 51, 59, 60, 61, 77
reliability, 2
religion, 49
reserves, 13, 15, 16, 17, 18, 19, 21, 22, 38, 39,
    42, 56
residential, 67
resources, 42
retained earnings, 34
retirement, 7, 17, 59, 69, 70, 71
retirement age, 70
return on total assets, 27
returns, 16, 49, 58, 63, 70
revenue, 56
risk, 2, 17, 18, 25, 27, 49, 52, 54, 56, 57, 59
risks, 25, 52, 56
RMA, 50, 51
robberies, 25
rural, 72
rural areas, 72

S

SA, 23, 28, 58
salaries, 70
sales, 12, 56

Saudi Arabia, 2, 9, 10, 11, 14, 15, 16, 22, 27,
    28, 30, 31, 32, 33, 47, 49, 50, 51, 53, 54,
    57, 58, 60, 61, 63, 67, 71, 72
savings, 11, 34
school, 11
SD, 10
secret, 31
securities, 1, 4, 5, 6, 8, 11, 13, 16, 17, 18, 27,
    31, 33, 42, 43, 53, 54, 55, 56, 58, 61, 63,
    64, 76, 77
security, 17, 30, 53, 54, 61, 63, 65, 69, 70, 71
self-employment, 71
services, iv, 1, 2, 4, 5, 21, 29, 30, 40, 55, 56,
    61, 67, 71, 75
settlements, 5, 8, 19
shareholders, 56
shares, 5, 7, 24, 42, 61, 62
sharing, 40, 43
shelter, 66
short run, 10
shortage, 3, 17, 25
single currency, 9, 10
small banks, 29, 68
social, 3, 4, 17, 54, 56, 65, 66, 69, 70, 71
social responsibility, 69
social security, 17, 65, 69, 70, 71
Social Security, 71
society, 7, 31, 54, 66, 73
software, 28, 30
Somalia, 15
spouse, 49
stability, 14, 19
standards, 25, 56, 66, 67
state-owned, 67
statistics, 14
stock, 2, 5, 8, 57, 61, 62, 63, 68, 69
stock exchange, 5, 8, 57, 61, 62, 68, 69
stock markets, 2, 5, 8, 63, 69
stock trading, 5
strategies, 19
students, 55
subscribers, 58
subsidies, 67
Sudan, 2, 9, 10, 11, 12, 15, 16, 24, 26, 31, 32,
    34, 50, 53, 54, 58, 60, 61, 72, 77

suffering, 32
supervision, 2, 5, 19, 25, 26, 48, 52, 56, 69
supervisor, 48
suppliers, 34
supply, 11, 67
surplus, 59
Switzerland, 19, 52
Syria, 2, 9, 10, 14, 15, 16, 17, 24, 28, 29, 31,
    34, 47, 50, 53, 58, 72, 73, 76
systematic, 56
systems, 9, 11, 28, 29, 30, 33, 48, 67, 68, 70

T

technical assistance, 19, 39
technical efficiency, 58
technology, 29, 66
terrorism, 31
terrorists, 31
theft, 48
third party, 66
time, 23, 27, 29, 49, 52, 61, 65
top management, 30
total revenue, 56
trade, 5, 68
trading, 4, 5, 14, 16, 17, 39, 54, 56, 61, 62, 68,
    69
traffic, 31, 32
transactions, 3, 13, 16, 17, 29, 30, 31, 56, 59,
    66, 69
transfer, 12, 29, 30
transparency, 25
transportation, 40
travel, 48, 68
Treasury, 6
Treasury bills, 6
trend, 69
trust, 30
Tunisia, 2, 9, 10, 14, 15, 17, 24, 27, 29, 32,
    33, 50, 53, 54, 58, 65, 67, 71, 72, 73

U

U.S. dollar, 9

UK, 50, 77
unions, 7
United Arab Emirates (UAE), 2, 8, 9, 10, 15,
16, 19, 22, 23, 24, 27, 28, 31, 32, 33, 40,
50, 53, 54, 58, 61, 63, 69, 71
United Nations, 39
users, 32

websites, 30
withdrawal, 43
witnesses, 66
women, 39, 72
workers, 69, 70
World Bank, 14, 23, 24, 27, 29, 30, 32, 33, 34,
42, 43, 49, 67, 72

V

values, 2, 9, 11, 18, 42, 60, 61, 63
vehicles, 59
volatility, 5

Y

Yemen, 2, 9, 10, 15, 16, 28, 31, 32, 33, 34, 72,
73

Z

Zakat, 56

W

Washington, 19
weakness, 32, 49, 52
web, 30